DIVINE
REVELATION

John Meacham

DIVINE
REVELATION

a call from Christ to join the armies of Heaven

TATE PUBLISHING & *Enterprises*

Published by Tate Publishing & Enterprises, LLC
127 E. Trade Center Terrace | Mustang, Oklahoma 73064 USA
1.888.361.9473 | www.tatepublishing.com

Tate Publishing is committed to excellence in the publishing industry. The company reflects the philosophy established by the founders, based on Psalm 68:11,
"The Lord gave the word and great was the company of those who published it."

Book design copyright © 2011 by Tate Publishing, LLC. All rights reserved.
Cover design by Blake Brasor
Interior design by Christina Hicks

Published in the United States of America

ISBN: 978-1-61346-086-3
1. Religion / Christian Life / General
2. Biography & Autobiography / Religious
11.05.18

Eternal thanks to Helen Cook for her uplifting faith in the Lord, for her constant encouragement to me, and for her tireless help on *Divine Revelation: A Call from Christ to Join the Armies of Heaven.*

Eternal thanks to Larry J. Leech II for his infectious love of God's Word, for his wonderful writing ability, and for his spiritually inspired work on *Divine Revelation: A Call from Christ to Join the Armies of Heaven.*

TABLE OF
CONTENTS

PROLOGUE

During my morning devotions on February 19, 2009, the Holy Spirit led me to the following passage in Ezekiel 2:5: "Whether those rebels listen to you or not, they will know that a prophet has been among them."

This book is my response to this directive from the Lord. Hence, the title *Divine Revelation: A Call from Christ to Join the Armies of Heaven.*

FOREWORD

The Christian life is a work in progress. Imagine for a moment if our lives weren't. Imagine what it would be like to know in this very instant all the remaining plans God had for you. How would you handle the information? More than likely you'd be overwhelmed. Maybe you'd hide in a closet or cower in terror under the bed.

God's plans are so incredibly huge for us that He can only reveal them a little at a time. Otherwise, we more than likely would freak out. His plans are far greater than anyone can ever imagine. His plans are often so far out of reach that you might scoff at the possibility of them coming to pass.

In *Divine Revelation: A Call from Christ to Join the Armies of Heaven*, John Meacham shares God's unfolding plan for his life through numerous revelations the Lord has given him since the early 1980s when John turned away from a backslidden life. Before that, John was a man of the world.

Then he started hearing what the Holy Spirit said to him during his morning devotions. For those who believe God speaks directly to us in these modern times, He does so in multiple ways. Many may think this is a little odd or just downright crazy. Maybe the problem is that we aren't willing to put down our agenda and truly listen.

The Holy Spirit teaches us. In John 14:26 we read, "The Helper, the Holy Spirit, whom the Father will send in my name, will teach you everything and make you remember all that I have told you." Jesus said this to the apostles because they enjoyed a front row seat to His life, and He was trying to help them understand they would have a new teacher after he ascended back to His throne in heaven.

Jesus also shared this, in regards to the Holy Spirit being a messenger:

> When, however, the Spirit comes, who reveals the truth about God, he will lead you into all the truth. He will not speak on his own authority, but he will speak of what he hears and will tell you of things to come. He will give me glory, because he will take what I say and tell it to you.
>
> John 16:13–14

With the guiding of the Holy Spirit, John has become a warrior in the army of Christ. John is a passionate man. You might say that he can be like a crazy man obsessed with finding an unseen friend. But for good reason, a faithful, obedient person following the calling of the Holy Spirit, he shares these divine revelations with for you for the single purpose of drawing you closer to God—your Lord, your Savior.

John Meacham

Some of the experiences you'll read about shortly might curl your hair or cause the hair on your arms to stand on end. That's not the purpose of sharing the story. In John's vulnerability of sharing these stories, you get to see the heart of a man who loves Jesus. With every molecule of his being, he wants you to experience the same depth of love for Jesus Christ.

John is also passionate about getting the church off its lazy butt. The church today, he feels, often preaches the wrong message or waters down the message. Both make his blood curdle.

Since being born again on October 24, 1982, John's life has never been the same. He hopes that in reading *Divine Revelation: A Call from Christ to Join the Armies of Heaven*, neither will yours. He hopes that you become on fire for the Lord. He hopes that you begin to better understand the beckoning of the Holy Spirit. He hopes that you will become more serious about your walk with the Lord. He hopes you will enlist in Christ's army. And he hopes to join you singing in heaven someday.

All his life, John has wanted to go to heaven, even during the time when his life certainly wasn't Christlike. During the first few months after giving over his life to the Lord, John received three hard-hitting and life-changing instructions. You'll read about them in the first few chapters. The third, received January 7, 1983, was a mandate for John to take a message to the world. That message is: *reflect the light*.

In these pages, you will realize that from his heart-felt words and by the guidance of the Holy Spirit; John does indeed reflect the light. In doing so, he is shining the beacon of Jesus Christ into a darkened world.

You might be part of the world, or you may have stepped recently from the darkness and are seeking. You also could be a seasoned veteran of walking with the Lord. Whatever background you come from, *Divine Revelation: A Call from Christ to Join the Armies of Heaven* will encourage and enlighten you. Inspire and invigorate you.

Ever the faithful and obedient servant, John shares these experiences to help draw you into a much deeper relationship with the Lord, one in which He can communicate with you on a similar level, and, hopefully, you will enjoy a lifetime of divine revelations.

—Larry J. Leech II
Executive Chairman,
Christian Writers Guild Word Weavers

John Meacham

BORN AGAIN

The Jewish leader Nicodemus, who belonged to the party of the Pharisees, went one night to Jesus and said, "Rabbi, we know that you are a teacher sent by God. No one could perform the miracles you are doing unless God were with him."

Jesus answered, "I am telling you the truth: no one can see the kingdom of God without being born again."

"How can a grown man be born again?" Nicodemus asked. "He certainly cannot enter his mother's womb and be born a second time!"

"I am telling you the truth," replied Jesus, "that no one can enter the kingdom of God without being born of water and the Spirit. A person is born physically of human parents, but is born spiritually of the Spirit. Do not be surprised because I tell you that you all must be born again. The wind blows wherever it wishes; you hear the sound it makes, but you do not know where it comes from or where it is going. It is like that with everyone who is born of the Spirit."

John 3:1–8

The doorbell rang at seven o'clock on September 19, 1982. I opened the front door of our home on Wildleaf Court in Charlotte, North Carolina, to find a policeman standing on the porch.

He asked if he could come in. Of course, I said yes.

His visit made me nervous. I had been jailed twice, so my history with police was not good. We went inside and sat at our kitchen table. He told my wife and me of a hit-and-run two weeks before on Independence Boulevard. The policeman said a woman claimed a car struck her car from behind, backed up, changed lanes, pulled around her, and sped off. He then dropped a bomb.

"The license plate number she filed in her warrant belongs to the gray-and-blue Buick parked in your driveway," he said.

"I did not have a wreck on Independence Boulevard!" I said. "And if you don't believe me, we can go look at my car, and you can see that there is not a scratch on my front bumper or a mark on any part of the car."

I went outside with the officer to examine the car. We agreed it had not been involved in an accident and went back inside. He called his sergeant. My wife and I sat nervously listening as he described the situation. We became concerned when he said, "But he has a wife and two children, and they seem like very nice people."

After completing the conversation and hanging up the telephone, the policeman explained that a hit-and-run is a felony. He instructed me to follow him to the

John Meacham

police station to complete some paperwork before the case could be closed.

My worst nightmare came true when we arrived at the station. After parking our cars, the officer took me to the magistrate, who stated, "Mr. Meacham, this lady has accused you of a felony hit-and-run and we have no choice but to place you under arrest."

The bailiff led me to the jail cell and, for the third time in my life, I watched the bars close in my face. Thankfully, my father bailed me out that night.

A few weeks later I suffered an anxiety attack. The stress from work and the suffocating fear caused by the possibility of going to prison nearly killed me. In bed that night my body went numb a little at a time. Starting in my feet, the numbness worked its way up my body until it reached my face and my eyes snapped shut. I thought I would die.

My wife panicked. She raced around the house trying to decide what she should do. Finally, she called my father, and he called 9-1-1.

When the ambulance arrived, I couldn't speak, couldn't see, or move any part of my body. My heart pounded out 150 beats per minute. The paramedics placed me on the gurney, put me in the ambulance, and drove me to the hospital.

My father rode in the ambulance with me while my now calmer but worried wife stayed home to care for our two sons. After a few hours of treatment, my pulse returned to normal, the numbness wore off, and I was released to go home.

My thirty-first birthday, October 22, 1982, was a week away, and my life was out of control.

The year before, my thirtieth birthday celebration included a surprise birthday party and lots of fighting with my wife. I hated surprise parties and gave her specific instructions not to allow our best friends to give me a party. She couldn't convince them to cancel the party. As a result, I accused her of not standing up for my wishes. We fought the entire weekend until my father stepped in. He convinced me of my foolishness, and I apologized to my wife.

For my thirty-first birthday, my wife cooked spaghetti, baked a birthday cake, and sang "Happy Birthday" with the boys.

Two days later, on October 24, 1982, I was born again.

In the shower that morning, I asked God to take control of my out-of-control life. The fear of going to prison and haunting thoughts of my recent anxiety attack consumed my mind, and I could not control my life at home or at work. While curled in a fetal position on the shower floor and as the water fell over me, the Holy Spirit entered me. And I experienced a new birth.

Knowing I must relinquish total control of my life to God, I started a routine each morning that included prayer, meditation, and Bible study. I didn't know where God would lead me, but I thanked Him for taking the reigns of my life and guiding me down His path.

A couple of days later, my attorney called to inform me that my accuser agreed to settle the case if I did not want to go to court the next day. I again proclaimed my innocence but told him that I wanted to pray about my decision and would call him the next morning.

John Meacham

During my devotions the next morning, I asked God what I should do. The Holy Spirit led me to take hold of my Bible by the spine, watch where the pages parted, to open the Bible at the parted pages, and to look for my instructions from the Lord on that page.

I followed the Holy Spirit's directions, and the pages parted to the section in the New Testament where Jesus told the crowd gathered for the Sermon on the Mount: "If someone brings a lawsuit against you and takes you to court, settle the dispute with him while there is time, before you get to court. Once you are there, he will turn you over to the judge, who will hand you over to the police, and you will be put in jail" (Matthew 5:25).

After thanking God for such clear instructions, I called my attorney and instructed him to settle. I wrote a check to my accuser for $150.00 and never heard from her again.

The next week, my recruiter placed me in a new job with an architectural and engineering firm in downtown Charlotte. I thanked God for my new birth into His heavenly kingdom and my new life in the Spirit.

Like Nicodemus earnestly seeking Jesus, I sought help after my conversion. After being born again, I met with my church's associate minister, Rev. Fred Holbrook, to seek his advice about my new spiritual life. He counseled that my focus needed to change from the things of this world to the things of heaven. When I asked how to do this, he shared that he stays the course with the constant reminder that Jesus directs us to "be concerned above everything else with the kingdom of

God and what he requires of you, and he will provide you all these other things" (Matthew 6:33).

Soon after, during morning devotions, God showed me three things of this world that I had to quit: cursing, drinking, and smoking.

I started cursing at age seven.

Neither of my parents cursed, but when I joined the Hickory Recreation Center swim team at age seven, I started hanging out with an older crowd. Mike, my thirteen-year-old role model, owned two national free-style records, enjoyed a flock of girls that followed him everywhere, and cursed all the time. So, in my first summer on the swim team, I did everything possible to be like Mike.

I had many other opportunities to let vile fly out of my mouth during my days as an athlete on swim, base-ball, basketball, and football teams. When I let a curse word slip out at home, I soon realized I didn't want a steady diet of bar soap.

My father, "Saint Hudson," cursed only one time that I heard. One Sunday afternoon, as he counted the money from that morning's church collection, my brothers and I reported that Cookie, our pet beagle, ran off for the sixth time in less than a month. My father spewed, "If that damn dog comes back, we are taking her to Uncle Jack's farm."

We never saw Cookie again, and I never heard my father curse again.

Unfortunately, I did not follow his example. By October 1982, swearing was a part of my everyday vocabulary. Now the Lord gave me clear instructions that I had to quit. To motivate me, I remembered my mother's wise words, "If you don't have anything nice to say, don't say anything at all."

Of the three vices the Lord instructed me to stop, eliminating swearing presented the fewest problems. I may have slipped up a few times over the past twenty-five plus years, but overall, my language reflects a life lived in God's grace.

At a company meeting some years later I witnessed this firsthand. A man whom I didn't know let an offensive word slip out in a group discussion. He immediately looked at me and said, "I am sorry, Mr. Meacham. I know that you are a Christian, and I hope that I have not offended you."

Stopping my drinking habit proved a more difficult task. I started drinking at age thirteen. During my childhood years in Hickory, my parents drank at their monthly supper club party and a few other social occasions but never at home.

My drinking started with my cousin at his family's vacation home in Blowing Rock, North Carolina. One weekend his mother went to Concord, North Carolina, to visit our grandmother and left us home alone. We found her secret bottle of whiskey, mixed at least three drinks each with orange juice, walked to the Blowing Rock Country Club to eat a cheeseburger and French fries, and vomited our way back to the house.

In retrospect, I wish this bad experience had soured me to alcohol. But it didn't. From age thirteen to age thirty-one I consumed more than my share of alcohol and experienced numerous episodes of drunken behavior.

Our minister at Amity Presbyterian Church, Rev. Fred Holder, preached one of the best sermons I have ever heard on the effects of alcohol on a person's behavior. He explained that God endowed each of us with "safety filters" in our brains that helped us screen out the bad behavior before the "bad thoughts turned into bad actions." Rev. Holder went on to elaborate that when we drink, the alcohol "punches holes in these filters, and the bad actions that we repressed before, break through the damaged filter, and all sorts of problems ensue."

For me this message rang loud and clear one Wednesday night in 1983 at our home on Wildleaf Court, when our youngest son came running into the house screaming that our oldest son had wrecked his bicycle and lay bleeding in the street. I rushed to our injured son, carried him to my car, and drove the two blocks to an emergency care facility.

The doctor strapped him to an immobilization board; the nurse grabbed his arms, and the doctor instructed me to hold my son's legs while he stitched up his wounds.

The night before my son's accident, I came home after a bad day at work, downed five drinks of Jack Daniels and ginger ale, and passed out on the sofa. Thankfully, the night our son was injured, I didn't have my usual Jack and ginger after work. I was sober. Later that night, I finally realized the long overdue need to stop drinking.

During my devotions the next morning, I asked God to forgive my procrastination in quitting drinking. I did not take another drink of alcohol for nineteen years.

John Meacham

The last of the terrible trio—smoking—began at age twelve.

My mother smoked about a pack of cigarettes per day during the early part of my life. She quit one day when I was twelve while she and I waited in my pediatrician's office for my appointment. There, she read an article about throat cancer and how the lady in the article could never talk again. That day, my mother decided she liked talking better than she liked smoking.

My brothers and I will never forget the Sunday morning after she quit. She rousted us out of bed early and told the three of us to clean the house before we left for church. She then started screaming about how lazy we were and that if we didn't get the house clean now, we could continue cleaning upon our return from church. The lack of nicotine taxed her addicted body, and I ran downstairs to seek relief from my father, who was working in his basement office posting the church pledge payments from the week before.

"Dad, you have got to come upstairs and help us!" I pleaded.

He looked up from the pledge cards, smiled, and quietly informed me, "You boys are on your own, and I would suggest that you go back upstairs and start cleaning."

I couldn't quit smoking until 1988, six years after being born again.

In 1985, Jesus indwelled me for a weekend , and those three days were my only smokeless days from October 24, 1982, until the day I quit on November 22, 1988.

The day I picked to quit was significant. I decided to quit on my grandmother's birthday in honor of her memory and in respect for her wish that I would not smoke. I planned to cut down from my normal two packs per day to ten cigarettes per day starting on my birthday, October 22, and then quit a month later on her birthday. I stayed on track with my plan until November 21. I smoked a pack of cigarettes that day and went to bed fearing failure the next day. I loved cigarettes.

In my devotions the next morning, I asked God for the strength to quit smoking. He gave me that strength, and I've never smoked another cigarette.

After quitting, I once told my wife that if I lived to be seventy-five years old, I would begin smoking again. I have since changed my mind. I cannot walk up my driveway without stopping to catch my breath. And during a visit to our house in June 2009, my granddaughter even asked, "Pop Pop, why do you cough so much?"

During a physical three months later in September, I registered zero on the oxygen scale, and I told my doctor that if I don't die in some kind of accident that my twenty-two years of smoking more than two packs of cigarettes per day would kill me.

Smoking proved to me that, "The wages of sin is death" (Romans 6:23, NIV).

I will not say that the path has no obstacles, but as with Nicodemus, my spiritual birth led to a new life of trying to follow God's will, and I still pray each morning that He will keep me on this wondrous path to His glory.

John Meacham

In my efforts to learn more about being born again and this new life, I read where William Barclay wrote,

> Nicodemus was a puzzled man, a man with many honours and yet with something lacking in his life. He came to Jesus for a talk so that somehow in the darkness of the night he might find light.
>
> Nicodemus is up against the eternal problem, the problem of the man who wants to be changed and who cannot change himself.

Barclay goes on to explain:

> To be born anew is to undergo such a radical change that it is like a new birth; it is to have something happen to the soul which can only be described as being born all over again; and the whole process is not a human achievement, because it comes from the grace and power of God.
>
> We then arrive in the kingdom of heaven. A society where God's will is as perfectly done on earth as it is in heaven. To be in the kingdom of heaven is therefore to lead a life in which we have willingly submitted everything to the will of God; it is to have arrived at a stage when we perfectly and completely accept the will of God.[1]

We see evidence of this new life in the Spirit from Nicodemus, when he risks his stature as a Pharisee and speaks out to the chief priests who wanted to crucify Jesus. He shows great courage when he defends Jesus' rights and states, "According to our Law we cannot condemn people before hearing them and finding out what they have done" (John 7:51).

We learn of more evidence of this new life in the Spirit when we read that after Jesus's death on the cross:

> Nicodemus, who at first had gone to see Jesus at night, went with Joseph of Arimathea, taking with him about one hundred pounds of spices, a mixture of myrrh and aloes. The two men took Jesus' body and wrapped it in linen cloths with spices according to the Jewish custom of preparing a body for burial. There was a garden in the place where Jesus had been put to death, and in it there was a new tomb where no one had ever been buried. Since it was the day before the Sabbath and because the tomb was close by, they placed Jesus' body there.
>
> John 19:39–42

In these passages, Nicodemus presents convincing evidence of following God's will by risking all that he has, using his resources for the kingdom of God, and carrying God's Son from the cross to the grave.

As a lay preacher during an ASP (Appalacia Service Project) mission trip to Panther, West Virginia, in June 1997, I shared with all ten teams (one from our church, four from Minnesota, and five from Texas) that after

John Meacham

being born again, Nicodemus became a different person, noting the following significant differences in his life after he encountered Jesus:

- He changed from spiritually lost to found by his Savior, thus changing his final destination from hell to heaven.
- He took risks for Jesus. When he sought an audience with Jesus at night, he risked his position in the Sanhedrin—spiritual leaders who hated Jesus.
- He orally defended Jesus in the Sanhedrin after they demanded Jesus' arrest in the temple where He was teaching the people contrary to Judaism.
- He displayed his great love for Jesus by helping Joseph of Arimathea take Jesus' body down from the cross and carrying Him to Joseph's garden tomb.

I made it clear that after our week in the hills of West Virginia, each person was different. We all changed, some more than others, from the person we were when we arrived. Now it was time for each of us to return to our churches and speak up for Jesus, just as Nicodemus did. We needed to take Christ from this place and carry His mission into our communities.

Like Nicodemus, some of the professing Christian workers were born again during this mission trip. Many others returned to their first love for Jesus, surrendering every part of their lives to His lordship over them. We returned to our home churches with a newfound love for Jesus Christ and new enthusiasm for His work.

From the 2009 American Religious Identification Survey, Jon Meacham (no relation) reported in the April 13, 2009, issue of *Newsweek* magazine that 76 percent of Americans say that they are Christians and 33 percent of Americans say that they are born again.[2]

Jesus cautions us, "no one can see the kingdom of God without being born again" (John 3:3).

Jesus goes on to inform us that "a person is born physically of human parents, but is born spiritually of the Spirit" (John 3:6).

Knowing that Jesus is telling us the truth, why do so many Christians in America not seek spiritual birth? Do these Christians shy away from spiritual birth because they seek a life of prosperity?

We live in a society driven by the American dream. Everywhere we turn we have a new target for our consumption: a new home, a new car, a new flat screen television, a new computer, a new cell phone, a new iPod, a new video game, new clothes, new furniture, a new vacation home, and, of course, lots of happiness.

A friend at work told of a preacher that showed her the way to prosperity.

The preacher showed her the way to find a new and better paying job.

The preacher showed her the way to buy a new house and everything else she desires.

The preacher showed her that she, too, could find happiness and live the American dream.

Now she starts every morning praying for a new job, praying for a new home, and praying for happiness.

Do these Christians avoid spiritual birth because they seek entertainment?

We live in a society that enjoys first-class entertainment: movies filled with graphic action and meaningful romance, television portraying real life scenes of danger and drama, radio proclaiming the voice of popular persuasion, music arousing our every sexual desire, and church worship services that offer the best show in town.

A friend at work told me of the wonderful praise team at his church.

The praise team employs a five-member band that features drums, guitars, horns, and a keyboard.

The praise team recruited twenty beautiful singers with the men and women paired together as they raise their voices in praise.

The praise team's men wear button-down shirts and tight slacks and the women wear low-cut tops and short skirts.

He loves to attend church on Sunday morning to watch and listen as the praise team proposes their gospel message.

Do Christians resist spiritual birth because they seek social acceptance?

We live in a society of unique individuals longing for social acceptance: whites, blacks, Hispanics, Asians, Christians, Jews, Muslins, Hindus, atheists, heterosexuals, and homosexuals.

At the Presbytery of New Hope's meeting to vote on the ordination of homosexuals, a minister came to the microphone and spoke against the proposal.

In closing, he opened his Bible and read where Paul wrote:

> Surely you know that the wicked will not possess God's kingdom. Do not fool yourselves; people who are immoral or worship idols or are adulterers or homosexual perverts or who steal or are greedy or are drunkards or slander others or are thieves—none of these will possess God's kingdom.
>
> 1 Corinthians 6:9–10

A woman later came to the microphone and spoke in favor of the proposal.

She told the gathered Presbyterians of her ministerial role in an area church, of her love for her female partner, of her love for her adopted daughter, of her desire to be ordained, and of her dream to baptize her daughter.

After everyone who wished to speak had spoken, the Presbytery of New Hope voted in favor of ordaining homosexuals, and the meeting closed with a prayer for unity and harmony.

Do these Christians reject spiritual birth because they seek knowledge?

We live in a society that affords limitless outlets for intellectual endeavor. Many an educated Christian seeks a life filled with mental challenges from school, work, and church.

John Meacham

I once attended a Bible study class on John 3:1–8 facilitated by an ordained minister who was not born again. As he taught, this educated pastor apologized for the confusing nature of the text and shared commentary from three well-known scholars about the passage but offered no personal knowledge as to the meaning of being born again. When he asked for comments, I shared my story of being born again on October 24, 1982. Upon hearing this divine revelation, the class fell silent for almost two minutes. To break the tense quiet, our most intellectual class member asserted, "We can all be like Nicodemus and ask Jesus to help us find more knowledge about God in our weekly study class."

Do these Christians fail to receive spiritual birth because they seek fellowship?

We live in a society filled with endless opportunities for fellowship. Americans enjoy countless hours of good times at football games, baseball games, basketball games, automobile races, pleasurable restaurants, and lively sports bars.

The theme song from the television show Cheers best expresses our desire for fellowship with the line "everybody knows your name."

In my book *Is Your Church Heavenly? A Question from Christ for Every Christian*, my co-writer, Dr. Lon Ackelson, shares this story from his call to his first church as a senior pastor:

> Each week that I visited people in the community, I faced persecution because of bad experiences the people had in my church

before my time. Sometimes the unpleasant experience was that of a relative or friend, but because of it, the person I visited refused to ever attend my church and they treated me as unwelcome in their home.

My enthusiasm to launch myself into the new community I served waned considerably as I encountered unexpected and unpleasant receptions in most of the homes in the neighborhood of the church. My church had a reputation that turned off many people in the community. The recent split involved a difference between the pastor and the board concerning his message topics. After the pastor said that *he* would decide what topics to preach, the board fired him. His current lengthy series had been on science and the Bible, and those tired of the series sought a different topic, but he refused to change.

He took about half of the church family (who sympathized with him) to begin a new church in a nearby school. At one home I visited, a lady asked me why she should go to a church where the people do not get along with each other. Another resident reported that people in a bar he frequented were better behaved than the people in my church were.

Lack of Christian recognition and unfriendly fellowship drives people away from the Lord, and understanding this problem, Dr. Ackelson closed his story by writing sharing that:

John Meacham

I learned to provide pastoral care when people of the community were hospitalized or bereaved. Over time, new people visited the church. As I was faithful to preach the Word and to live it, spiritual growth occurred within our congregation and the negative reputation of the church diminished.[3]

Do these Christians forget about spiritual birth because they seek long and healthy physical lives?

We live in a society obsessed with good health. Americans spend billions of dollars on hospitals, doctors, nurses, medical research, medical technology, drugs, vitamins, fitness, diet, and medical insurance.

Jesus enjoyed great popularity because of His medical miracles. He made a blind man see; He made a lame man walk; He made a woman stop bleeding; and He made a dead man live.

Thousands of people followed Jesus seeking healing from physical suffering or to watch the many miracles unfold as Jesus healed others.

Then some of the teachers of the Law and some Pharisees spoke up. "Teacher," they said, "we want to see you perform a miracle."

"How evil and godless are the people of this day!" Jesus exclaimed. "You ask me for a miracle? No! The only miracle you will be given is the miracle of the prophet Jonah. In the same way that Jonah spent three days and nights in the big fish, so will the Son of Man spend three days and nights in the depths of the earth. On the Judgment Day the people of Nineveh will stand up and accuse you, because they turned from their sins when they heard Jonah preach; and I tell you there is something here greater than Jonah."

Matthew 12:38–41

A Christian friend prayed that his wife would survive a head-on collision with a drunk driver. She died, and he never graced the doors of the church again.

Do these Christians miss the opportunity for spiritual birth because they seek security?

We live in a society consumed with financial fear. We fear doctor bills, mortgage payments, credit card statements, utility bills, the monthly car payment, checkout totals at the grocery store, the rising cost of college, and the ever-growing financial needs of retirement.

When America suffered financial crisis in 2008, Rick Warren proclaimed these money troubles brought people back to Saddleback Church in Lake Forest, California, where Warren is the senior pastor. And I am sure that many of them came back to pray for financial relief.

Nicodemus came seeking Jesus and when he found Him, he received spiritual birth and began a new life following God's will. After being born again, I found this same new spiritual life and now pray that every Christian will someday be born again.

John Meacham

GOD SPEAKS

The Lord has done this, and it is marvelous
in our eyes.

Psalm 118:23 (NIV)

For those who believe God speaks directly to us in these
modern times, He does so in multiple ways. Many may
think this is a little odd or just downright crazy. Maybe
the problem is that they aren't willing to put down their
own agenda and truly listen. I believe God speaks to us
daily. We just have to tune in. He can speak directly to
us through the words of another, or even in dreams, and
obviously through Scripture. In this chapter, I will share
a number of instances in which the Lord spoke to me.

During my morning devotions in November 1982,
the Holy Spirit impressed upon me to step outside our
home on Wildleaf Court. Although spiritually alive for
just three weeks, I knew immediately I should expect
something huge. When I stepped outside, I saw a fiery
cloud hovering over the house. The gigantic column-
shaped cloud was one hundred meters wide and three
hundred meters high. Inside the cloud, a swarming

mixture of purple, pink, orange, red, and yellow fire illuminated the predawn sky.

This fiery cloud reminded me of the story in the book of Exodus when God led the Israelites out of Egypt into the desert: "During the day the Lord went in front of them in a pillar of cloud to show them the way, and during the night he went in front of them in a pillar of fire to give them light, so they could travel night and day" (Exodus 13:21).

I stared, aware of the sensory overload, yet reveling in it at the same time. My mind cleared, my body felt light as a feather, and my spirit raced to the heavens to meet the Lord. As I soaked in the wondrous image above the home where my family slept, God said these words loud and clear: "Make it simple. Get it right."

Just a few weeks after receiving my directive to turn away from the things of the world (cursing, drinking, and smoking), my eyes and ears turned to the things of heaven and of being "concerned above everything else with the kingdom of God and what he requires" (Matthew 6:33a). I walked back into my house that morning with a direct command from God and absolutely no idea how to interpret those words. Confused, I allowed fear in. I thought people might question my sanity if I shared this divine revelation.

During the next few months, the Holy Spirit interpreted these words and directed me to simplify my life, seek righteousness, accept Jesus Christ as my Lord and Savior, and put God first. At the time, I was like most Americans with a life complicated by not enough time and too many things. Almost immediately I quit playing golf. I realized that being on the course each weekend took too much time away from my family and church. And I wasn't resting as much as I should.

This pruning process continues today. In November 2009, I read about Dave Bruno who "looked around his San Diego home one summer and realized just how much of his family's belongings cluttered their lives. So he decided to do something about it with a project he called 'The 100 Thing Challenge.'" Bruno said:

> By my thirty-seventh birthday on November 12, 2008, I will have only one hundred personal items. I will live for at least one year (God willing) maintaining an inventory of only one hundred personal things. This challenge will help me put stuff in its place and also explore my belief that stuff can be good when it serves a purpose greater than possession alone.[1]

I started with ties, which is no easy task. I love ties. When I first became a lay preacher in 1995, I began a habit of buying lots of new ties. I collected beautiful endangered species ties, museum artifacts ties, and, of course, religious ties. My favorite featured a painting of the Last Supper.

While researching the "100 Thing Challenge," I realized all but one of my thirty-three ties needed to go. I kept a gray one with green diamond shapes and these words written in red: "For God so loved the world that he gave his only begotten Son that whosoever believeth in Him should not perish, but have everlasting life John 3:16."

My favorite way for the Lord to speak to me is through Scripture. I love when He instructs me to open my Bible by holding the spine and letting the pages fall open to the passage He wants to share with me. I have done this countless times during the last twenty-seven years. While this may be strange for some, pastors have been known to belittle this method in their sermons. I find it soul-stirring and reassuring. Many books have been written on the topic of the Lord speaking to us, and I believe letting the pages of my Bible fall open to a particular passage is just one of many ways the Lord communicates daily with me.

This particular method was instrumental in shaping the direction and focus of Amity Presbyterian in Charlotte beginning in 1983. During my tenure as an elder at Amity, Rev. Fred Holder offered strong spiritual leadership, and Rev. Fred Holbrook offered abounding Christian love. Rev. Holder demonstrated his spiritual leadership by requiring that we obtain unity in the Holy Spirit in our session meetings before approving any proposed actions. Rev. Holbrook provided the session many hours of Christian fellowship on our elder retreats when he led us in song with his guitar and beautiful voice.

In addition to teaching Sunday school and serving as an elder, I offered Amity my God-given gift as an accountant and served as church treasurer and finance committee chairman. In 1983, I realized we had serious financial problems. Our expenses were up, our giving was down, and the fall pledge drive had come up over 30 percent short of our budget.

John Meacham

In this time of uncertainty, God revealed a new direction for Amity that focused our minds on spiritual development, rather than financial security for the church through the development of AIM (An Involved Membership), a five-year shepherd group program. We saw our church go from home visits of church members to solicit financial pledges (a worldly standard) to visiting members to offer a devotional Bible study (a spiritual standard).

The church committee asked me to work on the spiritual growth aspects of this new shepherd group ministry. Honored that church leadership would bestow this task on me, I shared my thoughts at the first meeting in January that we should focus our spiritual development on a theme Bible passage for each of the scheduled five years. From these theme passages, we could draw our stated spiritual objective, provide materials for individual Bible study, design class curriculum for group study, and emphasize the theme passage in the ministers preaching at Sunday worship. The committee liked this idea and asked that I pick a scripture text for our first year and report back to them at our next meeting.

In my morning devotions the next day, God showed me the Bible passage He wanted for the first year of the AIM program. As had happened in the past, the Holy Spirit instructed me to hold my Bible by the spine, look for the parting page, open to the parted page, and find the answer to my prayer. So I grasped my Good News Bible and saw the pages part to page 215 in the New Testament. On that page I saw written in bold letters: "Life in God's Service." I then read Romans chapter 12:

So then, my friends, because of God's great mercy to us I appeal to you: Offer yourselves as a living sacrifice to God, dedicated to his service and pleasing to him. This is the true worship that you should offer. Do not conform yourselves to the standards of this world, but let God transform you inwardly by a complete change of your mind. Then you will be able to know the will of God—what is good and is pleasing to him and is perfect.

And because of God's gracious gift to me I say to every one of you: Do not think of yourself more highly than you should. Instead, be modest in your thinking, and judge yourself according to the amount of faith that God has given you. We have many parts in the one body, and all these parts have different functions. In the same way, though we are many, we are one body in union with Christ, and we are all joined to each other as different parts of one body. So we are to use our different gifts in accordance with the grace that God has given us. If our gift is to speak God's message, we should do it according to the faith that we have; if it is to serve, we should serve; if it is to teach, we should teach; if it is to encourage others, we should do so. Whoever shares with others should do it generously; whoever has authority should work hard; whoever shows kindness to others should do it cheerfully.

John Meacham

Love must be completely sincere. Hate what is evil, hold on to what is good. Love one another warmly as Christians, and be eager to show respect for one another. Work hard and do not be lazy. Serve the Lord with a heart full of devotion. Let your hope keep you joyful, be patient in your troubles, and pray at all times. Share your belongings with your needy fellow Christians, and open your homes to strangers.

Ask God to bless those who persecute you—yes, ask him to bless, not to curse. Be happy with those who are happy, weep with those who weep. Have the same concern for everyone. Do not be proud, but accept humble duties. Do not think of yourselves as wise.

If someone has done you wrong, do not repay him with a wrong. Try to do what everyone considers to be good. Do everything possible on your part to live in peace with everybody. Never take revenge, my friends, but instead let God's anger do it. For the scripture says, "I will take revenge, I will pay back, says the Lord." Instead, as the scripture says: "If your enemies are hungry, feed them; if they are thirsty, give them a drink; for by doing this you will make them burn with shame. Do not let evil defeat you; instead, conquer evil with good.

Romans 12:1–21

For me, this passage drove home the point of God's command to: "Make it simple. Get it right." I felt as if Paul spoke to me on how to order my life and on how our church was to live in Christian fellowship. At our next meeting, everyone agreed that Romans 12 was a great first-year passage, and we decided on *Put God First* as our spiritual objective. The committee then asked me to pick the scripture passages for the next four years and be ready to share them at the March meeting.

We left pleased with the selection of this passage. Beginning with this chapter in Romans and through the first part of chapter 15, Paul outlines how the gospel transforms believers and the behavior that results from such a transformation. After devoting the first eleven chapters of Romans to theological discussion, Paul now explains how this theology works out in daily living. He describes how believers should live, not under the law, but under the grace of God. Following Paul's teaching, believers live in obedience to God, study the Scriptures and share them with others, and love everybody. The instructions in this passage laid the foundation on which we built for the next four years. It was important that, like Paul, we didn't put the cart before the horse.

Paul exhorts the readers to dedicate themselves to obedience to God, and that obedience is to be motivated by the theology just revealed. His exhortation is that they not be captivated by the foolishness of the world but would, through the wisdom of God, become pure and mature. In verses 3 through 8, Paul gives three practical examples of how the wisdom of God should affect one's life. The individual should be characterized by meekness as he recognizes his salvation is the result of grace. His meekness should result in smooth assimi-

John Meacham

lation into the membership of the body of Christ and result in opportunities for ministry which will benefit the other members in the body.

In my morning devotions after our second meeting, I wasn't surprised when the Holy Spirit opened my Good News Bible to page 126. There I read John's account in John chapter 3 of the night that Nicodemus came to see Jesus and was born again.

> There was a Jewish leader named Nicodemus, who belonged to the party of the Pharisees. One night he went to Jesus and said to him, "Rabbi, we know that you are a great teacher sent by God. No one could perform the miracles you are doing unless God were with him."
>
> Jesus answered, "I am telling you the truth; no one can see the kingdom of God without being born again."
>
> "How can a grown man be born again?" Nicodemus asked. "He certainly cannot enter his mother's womb and be born a second time!"
>
> "I am telling you the truth," replied Jesus, "that no one can enter the kingdom of God without being born of water and the Spirit. A person is born physically of human parents, but is born spiritually of the Spirit. Do not be surprised because I tell you that you must be born again. The wind blows wherever it wishes; you hear the sound it makes, but you do not know where it comes from or

where it is going. It is like that with everyone who is born of the Spirit."

"How can this be?" asked Nicodemus.

Jesus answered, "You are a great teacher in Israel, and you don't know this? I am telling you the truth; we speak of what we know and report what we have seen, yet none of you is willing to accept our message. You do not believe me when I tell you about the things of this world; how will you ever believe me, then, when I tell you about the things of heaven? And no one has ever gone up to heaven except the Son of Man, who came down from heaven."

As Moses lifted up the bronze snake on the pole in desert, in the same way the Son of Man must be lifted up, so that everyone who believes in him may have eternal life. For God loved the world so much that he gave his only Son, so that everyone who believes in him may not die but have eternal life. For God did not send his Son into the world to be its judge, but to be its savior.

Those who believe in the Son are not judged; but those who do not believe have already been judged, because they have not believed in God's only Son. This is how the judgment works: the light has come into the world, but people love the darkness rather than the light, because their deeds are evil. Those who do evil things hate the light and will not come to the light, because they do

John Meacham

not want their evil deeds to be shown up. But those who do what is true come to the light in order that the light may show that what they did was in obedience to God.

John 3:1–21

The committee loved this passage when I presented it at the March meeting. We also decided on *Born in Christ* as our spiritual objective.

To understand this story, you need to know two things about Nicodemus. First, he was a Pharisee. But he wasn't an ordinary Pharisee. Unlike most, Nicodemus was not a legalistic hypocrite who hated Jesus. Second, Nicodemus was a member of the Jewish ruling council. This was a select group of seventy men who served as a kind of combination Congress and Supreme Court. And the fact that he came at night indicates he couldn't risk being seen but also speaks of his great personal need.

In this story we see that Nicodemus admitted he had a need, went to Jesus personally, and trusted Christ completely. We must do that same thing. All three are essential in each of us being reborn. We must begin to apply this portion of Scripture to our own lives. By these words of our Lord, Nicodemus learned that entrance into the kingdom of God necessitated his forsaking much of the traditional theology of his peers, for the teaching of Christ. The kingdom was to be entered, not by the rigorous keeping of the Law and traditions of Judaism or by religious reform but by radical rebirth. This rebirth is not to be achieved by human effort but is the work of the Spirit of God.

A few days later when I asked the Lord for guidance in picking our AIM spiritual growth passage for the third year, the Holy Spirit parted the pages to page 132 in my Good News Bible's New Testament. When I saw the words "Jesus the Bread of Life" written in bold letters, I knew the committee would agree on this passage.

> "I am the bread of life," Jesus told them. "Those who come to me will never be hungry; those who believe in me will never be thirsty. Now, I told you that you have seen me but will not believe. Everyone whom my Father gives me will come to me. I will never turn away anyone who comes to me, because I have come down from heaven to do not my own will but the will of him who sent me. And it is the will of him who sent me that I should not lose any of all those he has given me, but that I should raise them all to life on the last day. For what my father wants is that all who see the Son and believe in him should have eternal life. And I will raise them to life on the last day."
>
> The people started grumbling about him, because he said, "I am the bread that came down from heaven." So they said, "This is Jesus son of Joseph, isn't he? We know his father and mother. How, then, does he now say he came down from heaven?"
>
> Jesus answered, "Stop grumbling among yourselves. People cannot come to me unless the Father who sent me draws them to me;

John Meacham

and I will raise them to life on the last day. The prophets wrote, 'Everyone will be taught by God.' Anyone who hears the Father and learns from him comes to me. This does not mean that anyone has seen the Father; he who is from God is the only one who has seen the Father. I am telling you the truth: he who believes has eternal life. I am the bread of life. Your ancestors ate manna in the desert, but died. But the bread that comes down from heaven is of such a kind that whoever eats it will not die. I am the living bread that came down from heaven. If you eat this bread, you will live forever. The bread that I will give you is my flesh, which I give so that the world may live."

This started an angry argument among them, "How can this man give us his flesh to eat?" they asked.

Jesus said to them, "I am telling you the truth: if you do not eat the flesh of the Son of Man and drink his blood, you will not have life in yourselves. Those who eat my flesh and drink my blood have eternal life, and I will raise them to life on the last day. For my flesh is the real food; my blood is the real drink. Those who eat my flesh and drink my blood live in me, and I live in them. The living Father sent me, and because of him I live also. In the same way whoever eats me will live because of me. This, then is the bread that came down from heaven; it is not like

the bread your ancestors ate, but then later
died. Those who eat this bread will live
forever."

John 6:35–58

Surprisingly, the committee struggled with this choice
and feared these words about the mystery of the body
and the blood of Jesus might be beyond the spiritual
maturity of our congregation. At one point, Rev. Holder
reminded us the study of this passage was two years
away and that we all, ministers and members, needed to
grow spiritually in these first two years of AIM. If this
happened, he was confident our congregation would
be spiritually mature enough to grasp the revelation of
these words. We all nodded in agreement and decided
Grow in Christ would be our spiritual objective for the
third year of our five-year plan.

The verses in John 6:35–58 contain some of the
most profound passages in the Bible. Jesus uses simple
language here to make his points. He's talking to those
who are hungry, not for physical food, but hungry for
"spiritual" food. These words are for those who are hungry down deep in their souls—people who have a sense
of something missing within them that physical things
would never be able to satisfy.

Jesus wants us to be satisfied internally, to have
that inner peace that many seek from various other
means, be it other religions or mind-altering chemicals.
Remember this most important fact: God loves you and
wants you to experience full satisfaction in your soul.

For the fourth year, God chose a portion of Jesus'

Sermon on the Mount when the Holy Spirit parted the pages of my Good News Bible to page seven in the New Testament. In Matthew's gospel, we read:

> "Make certain you do not perform your religious duties in public so that people will see what you do. If you do things publicly, you will not have any reward from your Father in Heaven.
>
> "So when you give something to a needy person, do not make a big show of it, as the hypocrites do in the houses of worship and on the streets. They do it so that people will praise them. I assure you, they have already been paid in full. But when you help a needy person, do it in such a way that even your closest friend will not know about it. Then it will be a private matter. And your Father, who sees what you do in private will reward you.
>
> "When you pray, do not be like the hypocrites! They love to stand up and pray in the house of worship and on the street corners, so that everyone will see them. I assure you, they have already been paid in full. But when you pray, go to your room, close the door, and pray to your Father, who is unseen. And your Father, who sees what you do in private, will reward you.
>
> "When you pray, do not use a lot of meaningless words, as the pagans do, who think that their gods will hear them because their prayers are long. Do not be like them. Your

Father already knows what you need before you ask him. This, then is how you should pray:

Our Father in heaven:

May your holy name be honored;

may your kingdom come;

may your will be done on earth as it is in heaven.

Give us today the food we need.

Forgive us the wrongs we have done,

as we forgive the wrongs that others have done to us.

Do not bring us to hard testing,

but keep us safe from the Evil One.

"If you forgive others the wrongs they have done to you, your Father in heaven will also forgive you. But if you do not forgive others, then your Father will not forgive the wrongs you have done."

"And when you fast, do not put on a sad face as the hypocrites do. They neglect their appearance so that everyone will see that they are fasting. I assure you, they have already been paid in full. When you go without food, wash your face and comb your hair, so that others cannot know that you are fasting—only your Father, who is unseen, will know. And your Father who sees what you do in private, will reward you.

"Do not store up riches for yourselves here on earth, where moths and rust destroy, and robbers break in and steal. Instead, store up

John Meacham

riches for yourselves in heaven, where moths and rust cannot destroy, and robbers cannot break in and steal. For your heart will always be where your riches are."

Matthew 6:1–21

The members of the committee believed this passage addressed the essence of our church's problem of too much emphasis on worldly issues and not enough emphasis on Christ's heavenly concerns. The committee unanimously accepted this selection and decided on *Live in Christ* for our fourth-year spiritual objective.

In the Sermon on the Mount, our Lord contrasted true religion with that popularly held and practiced within Judaism. He condemned the good works of alms, fasting and prayer when they were only done for show and not from the heart. Jesus also condemned the superficiality of materialism and calls on the disciples not to worry about material needs but to "seek" God's kingdom first.

While some have debated for whom the sermon was intended and how it applies, the truth of the matter is the words spoken are principles of how we are to live in Christ. In this day and age of many Christians seeking a life of flashy materialism, Jesus' Sermon on the Mount makes it clear that we are to have the proper motive for praying and that learning to pray in private lays the foundation for praying in public, giving humbly, thus eliminating the need to "keep up with the Joneses."

During my devotions on the morning of the March committee meeting, I prayed one more time that God guide me to our AIM spiritual growth passage for our final year. As had happened on previous mornings, the Holy Spirit parted the pages to page 145 of my Good News Bible's New Testament. My heart jumped for joy when I saw "Jesus the Way to the Father" written in bold letters. I went on to read of John's revelation from Jesus about His preparation of our room in heaven.

"Do not be worried and upset," Jesus told them. "Believe in God and believe also in me. There are many rooms in my Father's house, and I am going to prepare a place for you. I would not tell you this if it were not so. And after I go and prepare a place for you, I will come back and take you to myself, so that you will be where I am. You know the way that leads to the place where I am going."

Thomas said to him, "Lord, we do not know where you are going; so how can we know the way to get there?"

Jesus answered him, "I am the way, the truth, and the life; no one goes to the Father except by me. Now that you have known me," he said to them, "you will know my Father also, and from now on you do know him and you have seen him."

Philip said to him, "Lord, show us the Father; that is all we need."

Jesus answered, "For a long time I have been with you all; yet you do not know me, Philip? Whoever has seen me has seen the Father. Why, then, do you say, 'Show us the Father'? Do you not believe, Philip, that I am in the Father and the Father is in me? The

John Meacham

words that I have spoken to you," Jesus said to his disciples, "do not come from me. The Father, who remains in me, does his own work. Believe me when I say that I am in the Father and the Father is in me. If not, believe because of the things I do. I am telling you the truth: those who believe in me will do what I do—yes, they will do even greater things, because I am going to the Father. And I will do whatever you ask for in my name, so that the Father's glory will be shown through the Son. If you ask me for anything in my name, I will do it.

"If you love me, you will obey my commandments. I will ask the Father, and he will give you another Helper, who will stay with you forever. He is the Spirit, who reveals the truth about God. The world cannot receive him, because it cannot see him or know him. But you know him, because he remains with you and is in you.

"When I go, you will not be left all alone; I will come back to you. In a little while the world will see me no more, but you will see me; and because I live, you also will live. When that day comes, you will know that I am in my Father and that you are in me, just as I am in you.

"Those who accept my commandments and obey them are the ones who love me. My Father will love those who love me; I too will love them and reveal myself to them."

John 14:1–21

Rev. Holbrook loved this choice. He praised this passage as an enlightened way to end our five years of spiritual growth and proclaimed the final year should be a powerful year of evangelism at Amity. We accepted the passage and established *Open Arms* (later changed to *Conquer in Christ* to coincide with Christ's calling of the armies of heaven) as the spiritual growth objective.

We all face rejections, defeats, and failures that can create enough negative feelings to destroy us. In these moments we must be very careful. Often the most painful wounds are not the scars that are outwardly seen but the hidden wounds deep in the heart. Setbacks in our lives, struggles in the journey, trials that fall across the way can take the joy out of living. Our faith is weakened, and if we collect enough hurts, it will stop us from wanting to press forward.

We all have a tendency to worry. It's human nature. But we can lessen the amount of worry or fret by understanding what Jesus is saying here. This passage gives us hope and encouragement that we can overcome whatever the enemy has thrown at us. And believe you me, he will come after you, even if he hasn't already, and will continue to do so, often changing his tactics, until Christ comes to take His church home.

This gives us hope for the future. Ponder for a moment the depth of what Jesus revealed when He said, "I am going to heaven to prepare a place for you." For us, we can spend all of eternity with Him. For the church, we have the responsibility to ensure that everyone hears this good news and understands that our Lord and Savior Jesus Christ instructed us that "I am the way, the truth, and the life; no one goes to the Father except by me."

John Meacham

Because of this five-year program, the pastors, elders, and members opened the door and let Christ into Amity Presbyterian Church. The Lord transformed the church into a spiritually hot congregation. The pastors preached about "putting God first" and making Christ the core of our lives. They worked on practical Bible studies. They trained the elders in prayer and pastoral care. They followed the leadership of Christ—seeking to be good spiritual leaders of the flock of God. The elders at Amity, in true humility, surrendered their lay leadership roles to Him. They visited the sick and infirmed, delivered Bible studies to the homes of the members, encouraged each member to grow spiritually, and followed the leadership of Christ, seeking to be good examples to the flock of God. The members at Amity surrendered their lives to His lordship. They entered each other's home for fellowship, began to pray for each other, opened their homes to the elders, participated in a church-wide devotional Bible study program, and shared their faith with the lost, all because we listened and obeyed when God spoke.

Midway through the second year of AIM at Amity, I was fired from my job at the architectural and engineering firm. After four months of searching, the Lord led me to a new job as the controller for a John Deere equipment dealer in Garner, North Carolina.

R.W. Moore, owner of the John Deere equipment dealer, was the first Christian businessman I knew who actively practiced his faith at work. Moore arrived at work before six in the morning to start his workday with a devotional time of prayer and Bible study. He often told me that this time allowed him to let God direct his actions and the course of his company.

R.W. and his wife, Joan, secretary-treasurer of the dealership, shared their faith at work by offering a luncheon and Bible study in the company conference room every Monday at noon. In addition to the Bible study, the Moores hired Corporate Chaplains of America to offer their employees "Caring in the Workplace."

R.W. Moore's example helped influence me to co-author a Christian business book titled, *Helping Harry*, with Bill Barr. The book tells a fictional story of "Harry" and his management team as they try to lead their landscape supply company through difficult economic times.

In each of the book's seven chapters, the reader discovers the current circumstances of Harry's business, a Bible passage that God revealed to me in my morning devotions, and a series of commentaries titled "Christ in the Workplace."

I experienced the same parting of the pages for this book as I did when seeking the Lord's guidance for the five-year AIM program for Amity. The Bible story and the Christ in the Workplace commentary help the reader mature their faith at work by encouraging the reader to strive for a new way of life by portraying the image of Christ (John 6:35-59), challenging the reader to introduce a new vision of Christ to the people in their workplace (Acts 2:1-47), urging the reader to live a new life of faith, hope, and love (John 5:1-18), inspiring the reader to be brave and let the Holy Light of Jesus Christ shine through them (John 8:12-31), motivating the reader to let Christ guide them through the many crisis they face (John 11:1-44), offering the courage of Christ as the reader's way to calm the fears of the workplace (Matthew 14:22-33), and affording the reader a way to find their heavenly path and to share the peace of Christ with everyone they encounter (John 14:1-31).

After moving from Charlotte to take the new job at the John Deere dealership, our family transferred our church membership from Amity Presbyterian Church to First Presbyterian Church in Garner. I stayed active in the church for the next ten years, and in 1995 I received my Lay Preaching Certificate. In this new role, I preached at rural churches in eastern North Carolina, served the Presbytery of New Hope as Supply Pastor, became Lay Pastor at Plainview Presbyterian Church, and in 2003 was named interim pastor for Cornerstone Presbyterian Church, a start-up church in Cary. In this role, I was to walk this church to its grave, according to my mentor, because the Presbytery was tired of pouring money into an eight-year-old start-up church.

I didn't understand why. Cornerstone offered a lot to its people: a contemporary worship service, Sunday school classes for all ages, weekly Bible study classes, mission trips, shut-in visiting for the retirement community residents, community outreach, local service opportunities, vacation Bible school, and numerous fellowship gatherings of food and fun.

The congregation welcomed me immediately, and I knew that I couldn't take this church to the grave of dissolution before I asked God if He wanted them buried. Some time before my appointment as interim pastor, the church purchased property on High House Road in Cary with the hope of constructing a church building. So I drove to the property one Saturday morning and asked God if He wanted a church at this location. His answer was an unequivocal yes.

An ordained minister took over and led the church through the building process. Now today, more than 125 people worship God each Sunday morning in a beautiful church on High House Road.

In the prayer of invocation before each sermon, I ask God to fill me with His Holy Spirit and that the words of my mouth and the mediations of my heart will be acceptable in His sight. Only once in fourteen years of preaching did the Holy Spirit not come. On that Sunday, I nervously preached by the power of John Meacham alone and began to sweat. By the time I finished, my hands shook and the collar of my shirt was visibly wet. On the way home that day, I asked God to remove me as a lay preacher if I couldn't preach through the power of the Holy Spirit. I had come to realize that by working through me, and through millions of other devoted Christians, the Lord reveals His message to Christ's Church.

After traveling to Galilee and writing the book *Is Your Church Heavenly? A Question from Christ for Every Christian*, I again was blessed with seeing that through the completion and publication of this book that "The Lord has done this, and that it is marvelous in our eyes." Because of this experience with Jesus Christ in Galilee (see chapter 7, Christ in Galilee) and God's directive from my devotions on February 19, 2009, to follow Ezekiel 2:5 (see Prologue), I now describe my occupation on Facebook and on my business card as a "Christian Author and Prophet for Jesus Christ." In this role, I view myself much like the Wikipedia definition of prophet that reads "A prophet is an individual who has been contacted by, or has encountered, the supernatural or the divine, and serves as intermediary with humanity, delivering this newfound knowledge from the divine to other people." This definition fits me, because I believe I have a message from Jesus Christ for His church. But, and this is a very important thing to remember, I do not claim to have any specific knowledge of future events.

I have realized that "The Lord has done this, and it is marvelous in our eyes." More importantly, the things that I do each day could not be accomplished without His guidance and strength. That's why I spend my days following God's will and revealing His message to the world.

ACCEPTING JESUS

> For God loved the world so much that he gave
> his only Son, so that everyone who believes in
> him may not die but have eternal life.
>
> John 3:16

All my life, I have wanted to go to heaven, even during the time in my life when I fell away. While following Christ may not have been my top priority during those days, getting to heaven certainly was on my mind.

On December 10, 1982, I finally realized that everything I had learned about Jesus in church was true and that He was my only gate to heaven. The day before a street preacher gave me a Gideon's New Testament and in my morning devotions on the tenth, I accepted Jesus as my Savior and Lord and signed the following pledge:

> Confessing to God that I am a sinner, and
> believing that the Lord Jesus Christ died for
> my sins on the cross and was raised for my
> justification, I do now receive and confess
> Him as my personal Saviour.

The Lord revealed to me a number of things from this pledge: we must believe in the life of Jesus Christ, we must believe in the death of Jesus Christ, we must believe in the resurrection of Jesus Christ, and we must confess our sins.

In describing the life of Jesus Christ to the church at Philippi, the Apostle Paul wrote:

> He always had the nature of God, but he did not think that by force he should try to remain equal with God.
> Instead of this, of his own free will he gave up all he had,
> and took the nature of a servant.
> He became like a human being and appeared in human likeness.
> He was humble and walked the path of obedience all the way to death—
> his death on the cross.
> For this reason God raised him to the highest place above
> and gave him the name that is greater than any other name.
> And so, in honor of the name of Jesus
> all beings in heaven, on earth, and in the world below will fall on their knees,
> and all will openly proclaim that Jesus Christ is Lord,
> to the glory of God the Father.
>
> Philippians 2:6–11

John Meacham

In the biblical accounts of Jesus' life, I love the stories about His visits to the home of Lazarus, Martha, and Mary. Through His relationship with these three friends, we learn much about human and divine nature.

In Mary, we see the depth of people's devotion to Jesus. When she washes His feet with expensive perfume and dries them with her hair, we feel the warmth of her sacrificial love. Through Mary we also experience the human disappointment when Jesus did not come to Bethany sooner and prevent her brother Lazarus from dying.

From Martha, we experience the religious dilemma we all face between the necessity for human work in the church and our divine faith. While Mary sat washing Jesus's feet and soaking up His holy light, Martha cooked and cleaned then complained that her sister's carefree attitude was unfaithful to Mary's family duties. Jesus chided Martha and told her faith means more than work.

Apostle John's account of Lazarus's death and resurrection illuminate Martha's divine faith.

> When Martha heard that Jesus was coming, she went out to meet him, but Mary stayed in the house. Martha said to Jesus, "If you had been here, Lord, my brother would not have died! But I know that even now God will give you whatever you ask him for."
>
> "Your brother will rise to life," Jesus told her.
>
> "I know," she replied, "that he will rise to life on the last day."
>
> Jesus said to her, "I am the resurrection and the life. Those who believe in me will live,

even though they die; and those who live and believe in me will never die. Do you believe this?"

"Yes, Lord!" she answered. "I do believe that you are the Messiah, the Son of God, who has come into the world."

John 11:20–27

Through Lazarus, we see how people opened their homes and lives to Jesus. At a time when the Jewish leaders sought to kill Jesus, Lazarus invites Christ and His disciples to dine with him and his sisters. In the open light of day, Lazarus let the world know that Jesus was his friend and that He was always welcome in his home. When Lazarus died and spent four days in the grave, Jesus came to Bethany and raised him from the dead.

In raising Lazarus from the grave, Christ promises the same fate to all of those who believe in Him and yearn for a heavenly future after our human death. And Jesus warns that belief in Him and assurance of a heavenly eternity is not without risks. For in the gospel of John, we read, "A large number of people heard that Jesus was in Bethany, so they went there, not only because of Jesus but also to see Lazarus, whom Jesus had raised from death. So the chief priests made plans to kill Lazarus too, because on his account many Jews were rejecting them and believing in Jesus" (John 12:9–11).

During Jesus' life, the Bible reminds us that He is God's Son. Mark tells us that after John the Baptist baptized Jesus, He rose up out of the water, heaven opened, and God proclaimed, "You are my own dear Son. I am pleased with you." (Mark 1:11)

In the bestselling book, *90 Minutes in Heaven*, Don Piper struggled with his loss of a perfect eternal future when he returned to earth after ninety minutes in heaven. After reading about Piper's hardships, I can't imagine how Jesus could choose to come to earth only to suffer and die on the cross.

Imagine the choice for Jesus! He has been in heaven with God since the beginning of time and now God asks Him to leave the power and glory He enjoys in heaven for a life of humility and torture on earth.

And He said yes.

Jesus says, "Yes, I will suffer unbearable pain on the cross."

Jesus says, "Yes, I will sacrifice my heavenly home for a time of hell on earth."

Jesus says, "Yes, I will forgo my life in this timeless kingdom filled with brilliant colors to enter a dying world clouded in a lifeless gray."

Jesus says, "Yes, I will offer my life for the forgiveness of sin and the opening of the pearlescent gates of heaven to everyone who believes in me."

Why would God's only Son leave the perfect love of His heavenly home and come to suffer hell and hatred on earth?

Jesus constantly reminded His followers that He came down to earth to do God's will. As Jesus prepared to leave His disciples and be arrested by Pilate's soldiers, He said:

> The time is coming, and is already here, when all of you will be scattered, each of you

to your own home, and I will be left alone. But I am not really alone, because the Father is with me. I have told you this so that you will have peace by being united to me. The world will make you suffer. But be brave! I have defeated the world!

John 16:32–33

After Jesus finished saying this, he looked up to heaven and said, "Father, the hour has come. Give glory to your Son, so that the Son may give glory to you. For you gave him authority over all people, so that he might give eternal life to all those you gave him. And eternal life means to know you, the only true God, and to know Jesus Christ, whom you sent. I have shown your glory on earth; I have finished the work you gave me to do. Father! Give me glory in your presence now, the same glory I had with you before the world was made.

"I have made you know to those you gave me out of the world. They belonged to you, and you gave them to me. They have obeyed your word, and now they know that everything you gave me comes from you. I gave them the message that you gave me, and they received it; they know it is true that I came from you, and they believe that you sent me."

John 17:1–8

John Meacham

From the words of my salvation pledge, the Lord showed me that we must believe in the death of Jesus Christ. The Apostle John wrote this account of Jesus' death on the cross.

After the soldiers had crucified Jesus, they took his clothes and divided them into four parts, one part for each soldier. They also took the robe, which was made of one piece of woven cloth without any seams in it. The soldiers said to one another, "Let's not tear it; let's throw dice to see who will get it." This happened in order to make the scripture come true:

"They divided my clothes among themselves and gambled for my robe."

And this is what the soldiers did.

Standing close to Jesus' cross were his mother, his mother's sister, Mary the wife of Clopas, and Mary Magdalene. Jesus saw his mother and the disciple he loved standing there; so he said to his mother, "He is your son."

Then he said to the disciple, "She is your mother." From that time the disciple took her to live in his home.

Jesus knew that by now everything had been completed; and in order to make the scripture come true, he said, "I am thirsty."

A bowl was there, full of cheap wine; so a sponge was soaked in the wine, put on a stalk of hyssop, and lifted up to his lips. Jesus drank the wine and said, "It is finished!"

Then he bowed his head and gave up his spirit.

John 19:23–30

When Piper came back from heaven to earth to share a message about the power of prayer, he wrote many times that after those ninety minutes, he would rather have stayed in heaven than come back to earth. In heaven, he enjoyed love, joy, and perfection. On his return to earth, he suffered through months of pain and rehabilitation from his injuries in the car wreck that killed him.

After months of recovery and years of prayer, Piper found the strength to obey God's new plan for his life on earth. Upon reading Piper's book, you realize that in his obedience to God's will, we have received a wonderful gift—firsthand knowledge of heaven. With the help of Cecil Murphey, Piper's book reveals the glories of heaven, and their words give the reader a vision of the eternity that awaits those who believe in Jesus Christ. I knew Piper's story was a divine revelation when I read his book to my mother at her home on Lake Norman, about twenty miles north of Charlotte. The Holy Spirit entered me and forever placed in my mind a glorious vision of the eternal life that awaits me after my death on earth.

We learn from Matthew's account of the crucifixion that after the earthquake and everything else that happened, the soldiers were terrified and said, "He really was the Son of God!" (Matthew 27:54). In fear, they believed and turned to God's glory.

John Meacham

After Jesus died on the cross, Joseph of Arimathea and Nicodemus wrapped Jesus's body in linen cloths and buried Him in a new tomb.

Another revelation from the pledge is to believe in the resurrection. This makes sense. Without the resurrection, our faith is no different than Muslims with Muhammad or Buddhists with Buddha. Their deities no longer live. Ours does.

In revealing the events of Jesus' resurrection, the Apostle John wrote:

> Early Sunday morning, while it was still dark, Mary Magdalene went to the tomb and saw the stone had been taken away from the entrance. She ran to Simon Peter and the other disciple, whom Jesus loved, and told them, "They have taken the Lord from the tomb, and we don't know where they have put him!"
>
> After running to and checking out the empty tomb, Peter and the other disciple went back home. Mary stood crying outside the tomb. While still crying, she looked in the tomb and saw two angels dressed in white, sitting where the body of Jesus had been, one at the head and the other at the feet.
>
> "Woman, why are you crying?" they asked her.
>
> She answered, "They have taken my Lord away, and I do not know where they have put him!"

Then she turned around and saw Jesus standing there; but she did not know that it was Jesus. "Woman, why are you crying?" Jesus asked her. "Who is it that you are looking for?"

She thought he was the gardener, so she said to him, "if you took him away, sir, tell me where you have put him, and I will go get him."

Jesus said to her, "Mary!"

She turned toward him and said in Hebrew, "Rabboni!" (This means "Teacher.")

"Do not hold on to me," Jesus told her, "because I have not yet gone back up to the Father. But go to my brothers and tell them that I am returning to him who is my Father and their Father, my God and their God."

So Mary Magdalene went and told the disciples that she had seen the Lord and related to them what he had told her.

John 20:1–18

The resurrection of Jesus Christ changed the course of human history. In the events of this Sunday morning, we see God equaling the human roles of men and women. On this first Easter Sunday, we see the birth of a new world religion. And as John sees and believes, we realize that for all who hear this story and believe; Jesus Christ opens the gates of heaven and grants them eternal life.

For everyone who accepts Jesus Christ as their Lord and Savior, they experience the divine revelation that they are a citizen of heaven. From the moment we say, "I believe in Jesus Christ!" we are linked with the source of eternal love and light, and we immediately begin to experience the joys of heaven.

Less than three months after His death and return to heaven, Christ sent the Holy Spirit at Pentecost and gave His believers His church to enable them to experience God's heavenly kingdom on earth.

In his book *The Worship God is Seeking*, David Ruis describes the heavenly experience at Christ's church when he wrote,

> What makes worship truly Christian is its proximity. God is in the room. Worship is now not only objective, it is also deeply personal. Songs are no longer just *about* God, they are sung *to* God. Displays of adoration are not inappropriate but are a vital part of the worship's authenticity. Worship becomes about responding to God's presence. The dynamics of the liturgy change from that of a monologue to a dialog and response as the present rule and reign of heaven break through. God is here, and we will never be the same.[1]

One thing that stuck with me while reading of Piper's experience is that of the thousands of songs he heard in heaven, none were about the shed blood of Jesus. All songs in heaven were of joy and light. Not of Christ's pain and darkness.

During our choir's summer break in July 2009, our choir director called for men to volunteer for a special men's chorus to perform on the second Sunday in July. Lacking a trained singing voice but loving to make a "joyful noise" in church, I answered her call and went to our one and only rehearsal on Thursday night. I loved our first song, "Rise up O Men of God." But we sounded terrible. We rehearsed the song three times and kept getting worse, rather than better. Of our fifteen men in the chorus, only three could read music and, in my opinion, only five could carry a tune. As bad as we were, the choir director told us not to despair, and she assured us that on Sunday the Holy Spirit would be among us and would unite our voices for God's glory.

The man with the worst voice, ironically, who stood next to me in practice, asked how.

The choir director replied, "I do not know, but over the years I have seen the Holy Spirit work in so many people to bring so much glory to Christ and to God that I am sure it will happen again on Sunday."

She was right.

That morning when we stood to sing, the Holy Spirit enjoined us as we sang, "Lift up the cross of Christ! Rise up O men of God! Give heart and mind and soul and strength to serve the King of kings. Rise up, O men of God!"

After our spirit-filled performance, the congregation raved about our beautiful voices. And now the choir director plans to have the men's chorus sing at worship on a regular basis.

John Meacham

During my time as lay pastor at Cornerstone Presbyterian Church, I contemplated removing the Prayer of Confession and the Assurance of Pardon from our Sunday morning worship service. At a worship committee meeting, I witnessed a quick unity between warring sides of contemporaries and traditionalists when I suggested we drop the Prayer of Confession, the Silent Confession, and the Assurance of Forgiveness. Both sides asserted this time of confession and forgiveness was the most important part of our worship service and that their lives would be lost without these moments of cleansing and redemption. When I told the committee we could possibly go five minutes over our time allotment if we kept all three, one of the elders looked across the table and informed me that I could cut my sermon the five minutes needed to put us on schedule.

That night, I learned that we all have a basic spiritual need to confess our sins and to know that through our belief in Jesus Christ our sins are forgiven.

During the winter of 2009, I taught the *Is Your Church Heavenly? A Question from Christ for Every Christian* group study in the Ogburn Sunday school class at my home church of First Presbyterian Church in Garner, North Carolina. During our fifth session, we discussed Tolerant Thyatria Church and the need for repentance (i.e. the turning away from our sins). We talked about the sins of Jezebel, the false teacher who led the congregation in Thyatria astray. We also discussed the false teachers of today who lead people into sins of sexual immorality and idolatry. And, of course, we talked about our own sins.

As with the worship committee at Cornerstone, the class discussed the importance of coming to worship each week to confess our sins and receive forgiveness. As the conversation waned, I asked, "After we confess our sins and receive forgiveness, what should we do next?"

As I looked to the class searching for the answer, "We should repent of our sins," one of our oldest and most saintly class member raised her hand and said, "We go out and sin again and then we come back to church on Sunday expecting to be forgiven."

Her answer was a strong dose of reality and forced me to acknowledge that Christ's call for repentance, not only needed preaching at the church in Thyatria, but Christ's continuing call for repentance needs preaching from many pulpits today. I have to admit that in my fourteen years of preaching, I never preached a sermon on repentance. As a result, I realized that by not preaching repentance like John the Baptist, I had become a false teacher like Jezebel.

Unknowingly, I let our natural human desire for an easy life with no problems, with lots of worldly riches, with lots of earthly pleasures, and with Jesus' free ticket to heaven deafen me to the constant and clear call from Christ for repentance.

Many churches today are in desperate need of repentance, and they have intentionally locked Jesus out of His church. In September 2004, I experienced this dilemma firsthand when the executive presbyter of the Presbytery of New Hope asked me to serve as the supply preacher for Fairview Presbyterian Church in Selma, North Carolina.

John Meacham

Fairview had suffered a recent crisis when another lay pastor tried to bring this dying congregation back to life. She angered some of the long-time members and created a division between the local congregation and the presbytery's office. The executive presbyter was forced to mediate the dispute and released the lay pastor from her service to Fairview. Now, executive presbyter asked me to begin preaching there the next week.

After the executive presbyter told me of these unfortunate events, I agreed to serve this church. She instructed me to only preach at Sunday morning worship and that an ordained minister from Smithfield, North Carolina, would moderate Fairview's monthly session meeting of the church's elders. She warned me not to go to the meeting, not to introduce any new worship practices, and not to disrupt the comfort level of the five remaining people who attended Sunday morning worship.

In closing she said, "John, you need to remember that the church is not about Jesus. The church is about control."

Brothers and sisters, the church is all about Jesus, and He seeks reentry into His church. And on His behalf, I am the voice of someone shouting out from the shores of the Sea of Galilee "make ready the church for Jesus Christ!"

THE
DAZZLING LIGHT

The man took me to the gate that faces east, and there I saw coming from the east the dazzling light of the presence of the God of Israel. God's voice sounded like the roar of the sea, and the earth shone with the dazzling light. The vision was like the one I saw by the Chebar River. Then I threw myself face downward on the ground. The dazzling light passed through the east gate and went into the temple.

Ezekiel 43:1–4

During the first few months after giving over my life to the Lord, He gave me three hard-hitting and life-changing instructions. You read about the first two in the previous chapters. In this chapter I will share the instructions He gave me January 7, 1983, and the message God gave me to deliver to the world. That message is: *reflect the light.*

I share these experiences to help draw you into a much deeper relationship with the Lord, one in which He can communicate with you on a similar level, if He chooses. I share them to enlighten and—hopefully—inspire you.

That day the Holy Spirit led me outside our home on Wildleaf Court, much like He did two months prior. In the predawn sky, I saw reflected colors of purple and orange illuminated off thin gray clouds. On this cold winter morning, the sky seemed pregnant with a hint of snow but was overtaken by these colorful gray clouds.

I hadn't fully recovered from hearing God's roaring voice in November and feared what the Holy Spirit might show me next. We walked down my front steps to the middle of the front yard and then turned north. I shivered, mostly at the cold, but also at the sight in the sky.

A cloud formation that looked like perfectly formed gigantic black cylinders stacked on top of each other stretched a mile in length across the northern horizon. Each appeared to be approximately fifty meters high. Stacked ten high and rolling from top to bottom, this majestic cloud formation moved toward our house.

These clouds stopped rolling when they reached the treetops beside our house. Suddenly from between two of the cylinders, a glorious yellow light appeared and descended toward me. This beautiful glowing radiance looked like four one-hundred-by-one-hundred-meter diamonds, each with four sides and connected at their right and left corners. The entire dazzling light structure measured close to one hundred meters high and four hundred meters wide.

As the dazzling light flew toward me, I dropped facedown onto the ground in absolute terror. My body temperature felt much hotter than a 104 fever I experienced years before. I thought for sure I would die. Just before the light overwhelmed me, I looked up to see the dazzling yellow diamonds transform into an iridescent white Moravian star, which flew into our dogwood tree. Then just as suddenly as the dazzling light appeared, both the light and the dark clouds disappeared.

I continued to kneel on the ground, unsure whether I was dead or alive. The reality of the moment set in when the cold morning air enveloped my glowing hot body. I went back inside to the kitchen table to finish my devotions and Bible study.

"What did I see?" I asked God.

Then, as before when I asked about whether or not to settle with my hit-and-run accuser, the Holy Spirit instructed me to hold the spine of my Good News Bible, to watch for the parting of the pages, to open the Bible to the parted page, and receive the answer to my question.

I opened my Good News Bible to where the pages parted on page 380 in the Old Testament and read: "As the priests were leaving the temple, it was suddenly filled with a cloud shining with the dazzling light of the Lord's presence" (1 Kings 8:10–11a).

As these words filled my mind and the fever from the dazzling light heated my body, I prayed for God's grace in recovering from this divine revelation and

God's guidance along His path. The fever lasted about seven hours, but the fear still remains today after almost twenty-seven years.

From the rest of this passage in 1 Kings, we read,

> ...and they could not go back in to perform their duties. Then Solomon prayed:
> "You, Lord have placed the sun in the sky, yet you have chosen to live in clouds and darkness.
> Now I have built a majestic temple for you, a place for you to live forever."
>
> 1 Kings 8:11b–13

The revelation for me regarding the dazzling light is the importance of holiness in our lives. A total of fifteen scriptures in my Good News Bible are devoted to dazzling light.

So what is the significance of the dazzling light? What does it mean? And why are they important to you and me? Let's examine five passages.

Solomon was truly a man set on the mind of God and through his words in 2 Chronicles 7:1–3, we see that reverence for the Lord must be one of our aims in striving to achieve holiness. At the dedication of the temple, we read:

> When King Solomon finished his prayer, fire came down from heaven and burned up the sacrifices that had been offered, and the dazzling light of the Lord's presence filled the

temple. Because the temple was full of the dazzling light, the priests could not enter it. When the people of Israel saw the fire fall from heaven and the light fill the temple, they fell face downward on the pavement, worshipping God and praising him for his goodness and his eternal love.

From the scenes of the dedication service, we learn that in addition to reverence for the Lord, worshiping God remains a vital aim for a life of holiness. Many misconstrue that worship is just singing songs. Worship is much more than that. Worship is a way of life. I often think of what David Ruis said: "The rule and reign of heaven breaks through. God is here and we will never be same."

We also read about the clouds and the dazzling light in the stories of Moses and Aaron. In Exodus 16:9–12:

> Moses said to Aaron, "Tell the whole community to come and stand before the Lord, because he has heard their complaints." As Aaron spoke to the whole community, they turned toward the desert, and suddenly the dazzling light of the Lord appeared in a cloud. The Lord said to Moses, "I have heard the complaints of the Israelites. Tell them that at twilight they will have meat to eat, and in the morning they will have all the bread they want. Then they will know that I, the Lord, am their God."

From the desert experience, we learn God will provide for our every need and that a thankful heart reflects our aim for holiness. Ponder that for a moment. God will provide our every need. Everything! So why do we worry? Why do we fret over little things like our hair being just perfect? Why succumb to concern over whether or not someone likes us? Let God take care of us. Trying in our own flesh always, without fail, gets us in trouble.

In Leviticus 9:22-24, the day after Aaron and his sons were ordained as priests for God's wondering people, we read:

> When Aaron finished all the sacrifices, he raised his hands over the people and blessed them, and then stepped down. Moses and Aaron went into the tent of the Lord's presence, and when they came out, they blessed the people, and the dazzling light of the Lord's presence appeared to all the people. Suddenly the Lord sent a fire, and it consumed the burnt and the fat parts on the altar. When the people saw it, they all shouted and bowed down with their faces to the ground.

Here in this tent of worship, we learn that sacrifice displays a life of holiness.

As God's people continued on their journey in the desert, the Bible tells us of their constant complaining about Moses and Aaron. On one occasion, we read:

The whole community was threatening to stone them to death, but suddenly the people saw the dazzling light of the Lord's presence over the tent.

The Lord said to Moses, "How much longer will these people reject me? How much longer will they refuse to trust in me, even though I have performed so many miracles among them?"

Numbers 14:10–11

From the story in Numbers, we learn not to put our trust in people but to aim for holiness by placing all our trust in the Lord. This is hard for people. We want to trust but often can't. Human nature is to handle things in our own strength. How many times have we given something to the Lord, and when the slightest thing goes wrong, we take it back and try to handle it?

From Ezekiel's vision of the dazzling light returning to the temple, we read in 43:3–4, "This vision was like the one I had seen when God came to destroy Jerusalem, and like the one I saw by the Chebar River. Then I threw myself face downward on the ground. The dazzling light passed through the east gate and went into the temple."

After almost twenty-seven years of striving to live a life worthy of this vision, I have come to appreciate Ezekiel's never-failing obedience to God's directions. In that light, I offer obedience to God as another of our aims for holiness.

During the many times over the years of reflecting on my experience with the dazzling light, the Holy Spirit has shown me the transformation from the yellow light of the four diamonds to the white light of the multi-sided Moravian star symbolizes God coming into the world in the person of His Son, Jesus Christ.

From the experience on that cold Friday morning in January 1983, we learn the dazzling light of God's glory always shines above us. We should also remember the entry of Jesus Christ into the story of human history and see God revealing His desire to transform a sinful world into His heavenly kingdom.

Unfortunately, many Christian churches are going the wrong way. Many churches have driven Jesus Christ from their sanctuary and replaced the cross that hung above their door with a twenty-first century idol: the symbols for male and female. In this place you will find the worship of sexual pleasure consumes their congregation. At other churches, a smiley face brightens the doorway. Here you will find these congregations worship happiness. Other churches have hung the dollar sign above the door. In these sanctuaries the congregation worships money. A swastika guards the door of many churches that are controlled by a pastor who has expelled Jesus Christ from their church property. Thankfully, you can still find churches that hang the cross of Jesus Christ above their door, and through the power of the Holy Spirit their sanctuary glows with the worship of God.

God exposes the depth of the people's idol worship when Ezekiel wrote:

He took me to the entrance of the outer courtyard and showed me a hole in the wall. He said, "Mortal man, break through the wall here." I broke through it and found a door. He told me, "Go in and look at the evil, disgusting things they are doing here." So I went in and looked. The walls were covered with drawings of snakes and other unclean animals, and of the other things which the Israelites were worshiping.

Ezekiel 8:7–10

Many pastors today must believe that God does not see their human motives when they hang a smiley face above the door of His church. These pastors hold out the drug of happiness to a people who are consumed by personal problems and who hunger for meaningful relationships. These pastors then offer the church as the answer to all their woes and worries of this world.

"Come inside," the pastor says. "Listen to our wonderful praise team; enjoy exciting outings with your small group, and hear my uplifting sermons on the god we have created from the bestselling book, *The Shack*."

We need to remember the smiley face originated as the symbol for the drug LSD. Like LSD, happiness is a euphoric state that only lasts for a moment. Once the moment passes, we realize that not only are our woes and worries still pressed upon us, they have now grown worse because we deceived ourselves with a high of happiness that does not address the realities of a true Christian life spent following Jesus Christ.

Every week, more churches ignore the teaching of Jesus Christ and focus on money and its power by teaching financial planning at His church. By doing this, the pastor murders the spiritual life of the congregation with the economic desires of the church leaders. Sadly, this means more Christians worship money on Sunday morning than God. Jesus longs for these churches to take down the dollar sign from above the door, to return the cross of salvation to the gateway to God's kingdom, and to remember that He told us: "You cannot be a slave of two masters; you will hate one and love the other; you will be loyal to one and despise the other. You cannot serve both God and money" (Matthew 6:24).

> The Lord spoke to me. "Mortal man," he said, "tell the ruler of Tyre what I, the Sovereign Lord, am saying to him: Puffed up with pride, you claim to be a god. You say that like a god you sit on a throne, surrounded by the seas. You may pretend to be a god, but, no, you are mortal, not divine. You think you are wiser than Daniel, that no secret can be kept from you. Your wisdom and skill made you rich with treasures of gold and silver. You made clever business deals and kept on making profits. How proud you are of your wealth!
>
> "Now then, this is what I, the Sovereign Lord, am saying: Because you think you are as wise as a god, I will bring ruthless enemies to attack you. They will destroy all the beautiful things you have acquired by skill and wisdom."
>
> Ezekiel 28:1–7

Ezekiel reminds us that God constantly looks to reform the church when he wrote in 36:22–28:

> Now then, give the Israelites the message that I, the Sovereign Lord, have for them: What I am going to do is not for the sake of you Israelites, but for the sake of my holy name, which you have disgraced in every country where you have gone. When I demonstrate to the nations the holiness of my great name—the name you disgraced among them—then they will know that I am the Lord. I, the Sovereign Lord, have spoken. I will use you to show the nations that I am holy. I will take you from every nation and country and bring you back to your own land. I will sprinkle clean water on you and make you clean from all your idols and everything else that has defiled you. I will give you a new heart and a new mind. I will take away your stubborn heart of stone and give you an obedient heart. I will put my spirit in you and will see to it that you follow my laws and keep all the commands I have given you. Then you will live in the land I gave your ancestors. You will be my people, and I will be your God.

With the coming of Jesus Christ into the world, God gave all those who believe in Him a new heart, a new mind, and His own Spirit. In the world today, we find millions of people who follow Jesus Christ, and we can still find churches where the cross of Jesus Christ hangs above the entrance to the sanctuary. In this era of ever-growing idol worship, these faithful Christian churches must step forward and rally Christians throughout the world to take down the idols that appear over the door of many churches. They must make an effort to unite every Christian church under the flag of Jesus Christ, who is calling His followers to worship only God and to live a holy life as God's redeemed people.

Ezekiel draws our vision to the future when he wrote:

> This is what the Sovereign Lord says:
> I will take the top of a tall cedar and break off a tender sprout;
> I will plant it on a high mountain, on Israel's highest mountain.
> It will grow branches and bear seed and become a magnificent cedar.
> Birds of every kind will live there and find shelter in its shade.
> All the trees in the land will know that I am the Lord.
> I cut down the tall trees and make small trees grow tall.
> I wither up the green trees and make dry trees become green.
> I the Lord have spoken. I will do what I have said I would do.
>
> Ezekiel 17:22–24

Christians throughout the world must order their lives to live as the cedars of God, planted on His mountain and preparing themselves and the church for the second coming of Jesus Christ.

During my study of John 3:1–21 for the second year of the AIM program, the Holy Spirit instructed me to circle the number nineteen and to write "start B rock 2/23/97 9/19/97 reflect the light" on the margin at the bottom of the page. I wrote down these dates in February 1983. I made note of these dates and to wait for later instructions from the Lord. Fourteen years later I received my instructions.

During my morning devotions in January 1997, I returned to John 3:1–21 and read in verse nineteen, "This is how the judgment works; the light has come into the world, but people love the darkness rather than the light, because their deeds are evil." I sought God's guidance as to where He would lead me on February 23, 1997.

As I studied this note, I realized that "B rock" meant Blowing Rock, North Carolina, and more specifically, the rock in front of our family home in the Blue Ridge Mountains. The Holy Spirit then instructed me to be standing on this rock at five in the morning on February 23 and to be dressed in white.

My wife was upset when I told her of my plans to stand on the rock at the "Big House" (our family name for this property) to wait for a sign from God. That date also was the nineteenth birthday of our oldest son, and I would be four hours away when the sun chased away the darkness of the night. Her disappointment kept me from telling her I needed to buy a new white shirt, new white pants, new white tennis shoes, new white socks, new white underwear, and a new white belt.

After spending the night at a local Days Inn because the "Big House" didn't have heat, I stepped outside in time to make the short trip for my five o'clock appointment. I wished a white winter coat would have been part of my ensemble because the temperature dropped to twenty-seven during the night. After taking fifteen minutes to warm the car and scrape ice from the windshield, I headed out, nervous to see what God had in store for me. In fact, I was sick with diarrhea and my body shook with fear of seeing the dark clouds and the dazzling light again.

I parked my car in our gravel driveway, walked to the edge of the mountain, and stood on the rock at exactly at 5:00 a.m. I sucked in a cold breath. I gazed upon something that I had never seen in my forty-six years (my age at the time) of coming to the mountains. A full and perfect moon hovered directly over Grandfather Mountain. The full moon appeared ready to land on Grandfather's forehead. The mountain shimmered in the reflected white light of its early-morning glow.

I knew God's message—*reflect the light.*

God called me to share the vision of the clouds and the dazzling light with the world.

Upon returning home, the Holy Spirit led me to the Thomas Kinkade, painter of Light Gallery in Raleigh's Crabtree Mall. I contacted Kinkade about painting a picture of the clouds and the dazzling light. When he turned down my offer to pay him, the store clerk,

John Meacham

Chuck Pinson, who offered himself as a substitute, took the project.

After a rough first meeting to discuss the painting, Chuck caught the vision and produced a piece that we used to illustrate the message of dazzling light.

When I first saw the image at his place a few months later, I asked, "Where am I?"

He explained that while he painted, the Lord instructed him not to paint me kneeling beside the dogwood tree as I had requested. The Lord conveyed that this picture was not a revelation for my personal gratification but rather a revelation of God's glory for the entire world to behold.

How could I argue with that?

In addition to the original painting, which hangs in the Ogburn Sunday school class at my home church, Chuck provided a poster print copy to use for duplication and distribution. Over the years, I have made numerous copies of the painting, framed them, and given them to the churches where I preached and served. These churches have hung up their copies to symbolize one of God's answers to my constant prayer: that the light of His glory returns to Christ's church.

A few months later, on September 18, 1997, I drove from Garner, North Carolina, to Blowing Rock for my second trip to the rock to receive God's instructions regarding the reflection of His holy light. I arrived at about two o'clock. After meeting my best childhood friend for dinner, I turned in about seven hours later. At four thirty the next morning, I rose from bed, dressed in all white, walked off the porch of the "Big House," and stood on the rock. I faced Grandfather Mountain and waited to receive a sign from the Lord.

Exactly at 5:00 a.m., a perfectly full moon reflected the sun's light directly above my head. As I looked up, the huge moon appeared to be less than one hundred meters away. The mass consumed the entire sky above my head. I glowed in its reflected white light.

Now for the second time, God's message was: *reflect the light.*

In my morning devotions during the next few weeks, the Holy Spirit instructed me to reflect the light to more people by designing a website to share the picture of the dazzling light and to reveal God's spoken message of: "Make it simple. Get it right."

I responded by hiring a web designer, Stephanie Bledsoe, and we developed www.dazzlinglight.org. During my final day in Galilee, January 25, 2005, I received a third call from the Lord to *reflect the light.*

Having completed my writing on Monday, I returned to the Ohalo Manor and took an afternoon nap. At six o'clock I made what would be my final visit to the earth and stone stage. A spectacular full moon illuminated the night sky. I opened the windows of the car, turned on the interior lights, and read in Revelation where John wrote:

> Then I saw heaven open, and there was a white horse. Its rider is called Faithful and True; it is with justice that he judges and fights his battles. His eyes were like a flame of fire, and he wore many crowns on his head. He had a name written on him, but no one

except himself knows what it is. The robe he wore was covered in blood. His name is *The Word of God*. The armies of heaven followed him, riding on white horses and dressed in clean white linen. Out of his mouth came a sharp sword, with which he will defeat the nations. He will rule over them with a rod of iron, and he will trample out the wine in the winepress of the furious anger of the Almighty God. On his robe and on his thigh was written the name: *King of kings and Lord of lords.*

Revelation 19:11–16

As I read, a furious windstorm battered the inside of the car. At 6:21 p.m., my wrist-alarm sounded for nineteen seconds. I looked one last time at the earth and stone stage. I didn't set the alarm, so I considered it as Christ's farewell to me at this place. I then started the car and headed back to the Ohalo Manor. As I drove along the eastern shore of the Sea of Galilee, I was awestruck at the full moon reflecting the sun's light into the dark night sky.

When I returned home, the Holy Spirit led me to complete *Is Your Church Heavenly? A Question from Christ for Every Christian* and the accompanying group study guide as my response to God's call in Galilee to reflect the light. Recently, I began offering "Is Your Church Heavenly?" workshops to pastors, church leaders, and church teachers to discuss the information in Christ's re-issuance of the seven letters to the seven churches and

Christ's call for church reform. Today, my hope for the books and the workshops are that they will be God's answer to my constant prayer that the light of His glory will return to the church of His Son, Jesus Christ.

Unlike Ezekiel, I never saw the dark clouds and the dazzling light again. However, sometimes on the stormy days that I travel through Charlotte on Interstate 85, I will see the lights of a large jet descend from a group of gathering dark clouds over the Billy Graham Parkway as the jet approaches Douglas International Airport. For a moment I stare in fearful anticipation that the dazzling light of God's glory is on the verge of returning. After the moment passes and the memories return, I pray thanks to God for my experience in January 1983, and I ask Him to continue to guide my path until I see once again the dazzling light of His glory that forever illuminates our heavenly home.

John Meacham

JESUS SINGS

When the apostles met together with Jesus, they asked him, "Lord, will you at this time give the Kingdom back to Israel?"

Jesus said to them, "The times and occasions are set by my Father's own authority, and it is not for you to know when they will be. But when the Holy Spirit comes upon you, you will be filled with power, and you will be witnesses for me in Jerusalem, in all of Judea and Samaria, and to the ends of the earth." After saying this, he was taken up to heaven as they watched him, and a cloud hid him from their sight.

They still had their eyes fixed on the sky as he went away, when two men dressed in white suddenly stood beside them and said, "Galileans, why are you standing there looking up at the sky? This Jesus, who was taken from you into heaven, will come back in the same way that you saw him go to heaven."

Acts 1:6–11

How many times have you ever cried out to Christ, "Use me. Let me be your witness"? In that moment, you are most sincere. You really want Christ to use you. Any way He wants. You're willing. You're ready.

But does that feeling, that sincerity last? Are you as ready and willing right now, where you're sitting, as you were the moment you cried out to Him, or have you retreated slightly into a comfort zone full of cozy people and things? Have you been disappointed that being used didn't include being on the "big stage"?

But to be willing, truly willing, we have to be ready for even the small things. Sometimes the small includes the right words at the right time, poured into a willing vessel by the Holy Spirit in the middle of a conversation. When we are willing, we don't have to be on a big stage or a have a big platform. We just have to be willing.

Let me share a story from many years ago that drove home that point to me. In 1984, only a week after my third dream of the second coming, I dreamed of lifting out of a swing at Frank Liske Park off Highway 49 near Concord, North Carolina. I spent many hours with my boys at that park. Our play always ended up in the playground on the slides, monkey bars, and the best swings I have ever swung on. In my dream, I came out of one of those swings and drifted over the spotlights on the tennis court, over the lake shaped like the Sea of Galilee, and much to my surprise, up into the clouds to meet Jesus as He descended to earth.

Unfortunately, we never met in the sky. I only saw Him from a distance. To say I was disappointed would be an understatement. I was so close to being with my Lord and Savior. Yet I was so far. I woke up before we made contact. Consumed with uncertainty about how this dream would affect the future, I replayed the dream over and over in my mind before rising for the day.

During my morning devotions Saturday, April 6, 1985 (the day between Good Friday and Easter Sunday in 1985), the Holy Spirit gave me specifics instructions for Friday, April 12. I hope you've noticed while reading the first four chapters the importance of obedience. Yes, some things seem outrageous, both to others and you. *Crazy* might even be a word to describe the instruction or even the feeling associated with obeying those instructions. But we must still be obedient.

So I had my marching orders for that day. I left my office at the architectural and engineering firm at eleven in the morning and drove to Frank Liske Park. I parked my blue-and-gray Buick near the lake so I could pick up Jesus at noon—yup. Jesus in my car. I didn't know what to expect. On one hand I was excited, but the prevailing feeling was fear of the unknown.

The Holy Spirit informed me that Jesus would ride in the backseat. Why, I'm not sure. I wasn't told. More importantly, I was not to smoke or commit any sins in His presence during the three days Jesus would spend with me.

At noon, I felt the presence of Jesus enter the backseat. I looked into the rearview mirror, and the voice of Jesus said, "I am ready."

I drove out of the park, making sure I obeyed the unusual nineteen miles per hour speed limit. By the time I turned left onto Stough Road, the presence of His Spirit overwhelmed me. My body visibly shook with nervous excitement. To calm my excitement and steady my nerves, I lit a cigarette.

Big mistake!

Because of my disobedience, I coughed and gagged. My body shook in anguish. Just as I lurched forward to vomit, Jesus said, "I told you not to smoke in my presence."

I extinguished the cigarette and drove us to my home on Wildleaf Court in silence. When we pulled into the driveway and drove past the dogwood tree in our front yard, the spirit of Jesus exited the backseat and entered me.

My body felt light as feather, similar to the morning that I heard God speak. My mind was clear of my past and free of the burdens of my life. For the first and only time in my life, I felt that with Jesus indwelling me that I was without sin, and my spirit felt fully alive and in total harmony with God. I felt perfect.

That night, after we met my parents for dinner and put the boys to bed, I longed for a peaceful and restful night of sleep. Receiving Jesus' spirit, while exhilarating in the spiritual realm, wore out my human body. Feeling Christ's continuing presence in my soul, I tossed and turned most of the night. Finally, I got up at about four o'clock, an hour earlier than my usual time to start my devotions at the kitchen table.

As I felt the spirit of Jesus awake in my soul, I opened the Good News Bible to page 351 in the New Testament and read in Revelation where John wrote,

Then I saw heaven open and there was a white horse. Its rider is called Faithful and True; it is with justice that he judges and fights his battles. His eyes were like a flame of fire, and he wore many crowns on his head. He had a name written on him, but no one except himself knows what it is. The robe he wore was covered with blood. His name is *The Word of God.* The armies of heaven followed him, riding on white horses and dressed in clean white linen. Out of his mouth came a sharp sword, with which he will defeat the nations. He will rule over them with a rod of iron, and he will trample out the wine in the wine press of the furious anger of the Almighty God. On his robe and on his thigh was written the name: *King of kings and Lord of lords.*

Revelation 19:11–16

After reading this passage, Jesus gave me my new name and informed me that He would sing the next day during the eleven o'clock service at Amity Presbyterian Church. In Galilee years later, Christ gave me a white stone with the name inscribed on it, fulfilling what is written in Revelation 2:17: "I will also give him a white stone with a new name written on it, known only to him who receives it."

Saturday evening, we all went to a neighborhood party for the entire family. At the party, I noticed that, unlike me, Jesus had a boundless empathy and an enormous love for other people. In my world, it was all about me, but while the Spirit of Jesus indwelled me, it was all about others. That night, I spent time on the swing set with the kids and found myself humming the song "Jesus Loves the Little Children."

At church the next morning, I experienced His love grow a thousandfold as He consumed my whole being with His eternal love for His Father and His deep concern for His church. This spiritual experience reached its crescendo, when we stood in worship to sing "Eternal God, Whose Power Upholds."

As Jesus told me during devotions the day before, when I opened my mouth to sing, His voice proclaimed the words of this hymn. After worship service at Amity that fateful Sunday, Rev. Fred Holbrook, who stood at the pulpit just a few feet away from where Jesus sang in the second pew, said to me, "I heard Jesus sing through your today!"

"Yeah, I know! And He is still with me!" I replied.

Someone asked me to describe how I felt that morning. I said, "Take the most vivid memory you have of being filled with the Holy Spirit and multiply it times one hundred." At times I felt I was already in heaven, even though the pull of earth's gravity held me down. My body was also hot to the touch. I remember hugging one of our older female members after church and she said that she could feel the Spirit of the Lord upon me.

When we look to the words of this hymn, we hear Christ's message to every Christian and to His Church.

Eternal God, whose power upholds both
flower and flaming star,
   To whom there is no here nor there, no
time no near nor far,
   No alien race, no foreign shore, no child
unsought, unknown;
   O send us forth, Thy prophets true, to
make all lands Thine own!

I served as an elder under one of those prophets during
my time at Amity beginning in 1979. In my opinion,
Rev. Fred Holder, now retired and living in Montreat,
North Carolina, has always been one of Christ's true
prophets. When he stood to preach, you knew deep in
your spirit the message Holder presented came directly
from Christ Himself.

Many feel that Jim Bakker was one of the great false
prophets of the 1980s. On a Sunday morning in 1984,
The Charlotte Observer broke a story about Bakker's
Praise the Lord ministry's fraudulent fund-raising activi-
ties that would eventually lead to his conviction. Four
years later, he was indicted on eight counts of mail
fraud, fifteen counts of wire fraud, and one count of
conspiracy. A year later, a Charlotte jury found him
guilty on all twenty-four counts, and he was sentenced
to forty-five years in federal prison and a $500,000 fine.

When Rev. Holder stood to preach that Sunday
morning in 1984, he began by holding up the newspaper and showing us the day's headline about Bakker.
He then instructed the ushers to lock the church doors
and proclaimed he had something to say, that we were
going to listen, and that we could forget about being

first in the cafeteria line today. He then emptied his heart, mind, and spirit as he preached about all the evil that Bakker had inflicted on God's kingdom and then implored our congregation to reach out and help the homeless Christians in our community who had sold their belongings and given all the proceeds to Bakker's *Praise the Lord* ministry.

Rev. Holder's words that day still ring in my ears as the voice of the Lord speaking out against false prophets. For on that Sunday morning, he locked Satan out of our church, and his words brought us into God's kingdom.

Today, Jesus asks, "Where are those true prophets that proclaim my gospel on my behalf?"

Where are those true prophets that look to open the doors of heaven and point their congregations to God's eternal home?"

"Where are those true prophets who will lead my congregation in singing, 'Lift up the cross of Christ! Rise up O Church of God! Give heart and mind and soul and strength to serve the King of kings. Rise up O Church of God!'"

> O God of love, whose Spirit wakes in every
> human breast,
> Whom love, and love alone, can know, in
> whom all hearts find rest;
> Help us to spread Thy gracious reign till
> greed and hate shall cease,
> And kindness dwell in human hearts, and
> all the earth find peace!
> "Eternal God, Whose Power Upholds,"
> verse two

John Meacham

Jesus sings out to the church of today, "When will my church repent?"

If you do not repent, I will come to you and remove your lampstand from its place."

Repent therefore! Otherwise, I will soon come to you and will fight against you with the sword from my mouth."

I will cast her on a bed of suffering and I will make those who committed adultery with her suffer intensely, unless they repent of her ways. I will strike her children dead."

Pastor Ben Pomales often preaches on our need for repentance at Frontier Baptist Church in Angelton, Texas. During our group discussion at the "Is Your Church Heavenly?" workshop, Pastor Pomales said, "The Lord cannot use an unrepentant sinner." And today, Christ cannot reclaim His church unless sinners repent of the greed that rules our every thought and strive for the riches of heaven.

Christ cannot reclaim His church, unless sinners repent of the hatred and the prejudice that drive our lives apart and live for Christ's true peace.

Christ cannot reclaim His church, unless sinners repent of the countless church rules and regulations that bind the souls of Christ's followers and find the love of God's Spirit that hides inside our heart.

Christ cannot reclaim His church, unless sinners repent of our apathetic faith and glow spiritually hot for Jesus.

O God of truth, whom science seeks and
reverent souls adore,
    Who lightest every earnest mind of every
clime and shore;
    Dispel the gloom of error's night, of igno-
rance and fear,
    Until true wisdom from above shall make
life's pathway clear!
    "Eternal God, Whose Power Upholds,"
verse three

After being born again, I seek God's clear pathway
for my life each morning in my devotions. For me, the
trouble is not seeing the path; the trouble is staying
on the path after my devotions each morning. We
all face troubles with our families, conflicts where we
work, and temptations from Satan everywhere we turn.
However, we must strive each day, all day to seek God's
eternal truth, to dispel the darkness in our lives, and to
experience the peace of Jesus Christ in every moment.
Then as mature Christians, we can follow life's pathway
clear to heaven's door.

O God of Beauty, oft revealed in dreams of
human art,
    In speech that flows to melody, in holiness
of heart;
    Teach us to ban all ugliness that blinds our
eyes to Thee,
    Till all shall know the loveliness of lives
made fair and free!

"Eternal God, Whose Power Upholds,"
verse four

In his best-selling book, *Become a Better You*, Joel Osteen proposes that to become a better you, you must:

1. Keep pressing forward
2. Be positive toward yourself
3. Develop better relationships
4. Form better habits
5. Embrace the place where you are
6. Develop your inner life
7. Stay passionate about life[1]

I decided to read this book because I speak out against Osteen and the Prosperity Gospel in radio interviews. I feel this message is not a Christian message for one simple reason: a Christian message proposes a life passionate for Jesus Christ and not one for us.

Osteen doesn't preach a Christian message. In studying his book and noting on the title page the number one purpose was self-actualization, I realized he promotes some form of the power of positive thinking supported by an Old Testament faith-based financial reward system. I coined a phrase to describe this philosophy: "Joelism."

Today, Joelism represents a growing world religion with as many as 40,000 people attending Sunday worship at Lakewood Church in Houston, Texas, and more than seven million people receiving Osteen's false teaching via satellite in over one hundred countries around the world.

Contrary to Osteen's teachings of self-actualization, Jesus said, "Love your God with all your heart, with all your soul, with all your mind, and with all your strength" (Mark 12:30).

When we focus our hearts on God and not ourselves, we become better Christians and begin to experience the joys of heaven, sing the songs of heaven, find our way through the darkness of this world into the eternal light of heaven, and realize that we are living Christ's second commandment to "love your neighbors as you love yourself" (Mark 12:31).

> O God of righteousness and grace, seen in
> the Christ, Thy Son,
>   Whose life and death reveal Thy face, by
> whom Thy will was done;
>   Inspire Thy heralds of good news to live
> Thy life divine,
>   Till Christ is formed in all mankind and
> every land is Thine!
>   "Eternal God, Whose Power Upholds,"
> verse five

Remember the passages mentioned in chapter 2 pertaining to AIM, the five-year shepherd group program we started at Amity Presbyterian in 1983? The plan was to move people from their seats to an active life in serving Christ, to "inspire Thy heralds of good news to live Thy life divine, till Christ is formed in all mankind and every land is thine!" We moved through

John Meacham

Put God First to *Born in Christ* to *Grow in Christ* to *Live in Christ* and finished with *Conquer in Christ*. Many changes took place in lives, mindsets, and hearts.

Christ transformed those willing to change. Are you willing to be a living, breathing Christ follower? Are you willing to change? Are you willing to let God's light shine *through* you?

While it might be easy to say yes as you read the words, transforming, changing, and living it is a whole 'nother ball of wax.

Jesus continues to sing through me today at the "Is Your Church Heavenly?" workshops. These workshops are designed to bring the presence of Jesus Christ back into His church and to prepare His congregation for His second coming. To this end, Christ reveals in these workshops these seven steps to becoming a heavenly church.

1. Wake up

2. Repent

3. Open your doors to Jesus Christ

4. Be faithful and true to God

5. Strive for spiritual riches

6. Live with enthusiasm for Christ

7. Seek the lost for Christ

Christ calls out, "Wake up!" Jesus told John to write to the dying church at Sardis: "Wake up, and strengthen what you still have before it dies completely" (Revelation 3:2a). To help prepare His congregation for His second coming, Christ seeks 24/7 Christians who always demonstrate a living faith. Christ seeks Christians who will expel hypocrites from many of the church's best pews and will work to restore the days of fellowship and faith found in the early church of Acts.

Christ calls out, "Repent!" Jesus told John to write to the tolerant church at Thyatira: "You tolerate that woman Jezebel" (Revelation 2:20a). To help prepare His congregation for His second coming, Christ seeks to enlist Christians who are intolerant of sexual immorality and idolatry. Christ seeks Christians who will speak out against the sins of today and will help their brothers and sisters turn away from the darkness of hell toward the light of heaven.

Christ calls out, "Open your doors to me!" Jesus told John to write to the apathetic church at Laodicea: "You are lukewarm." To help prepare His congregation for His second coming, Christ seeks spiritually hot Christians. Christ seeks Christians who will open the doors of the church to Him and will light the spiritual embers of God's eternal kingdom.

Christ calls out, "Be faithful and true to God!" Jesus told John to write to the true and false church at Pergamum: "There are a few things I have against you" (Revelation 2:14a). To help prepare His congregation for His second coming, Christ seeks to train Christian soldiers to fight against false teachers. Christ seeks Christians who will fight against "those people" that are trying to lead His followers astray and will teach His congregation the truth of His gospel.

Christ calls out, "Strive for spiritual riches!" Jesus told John to write to the spirit filled church at Smyrna:

"You are rich!" To help prepare His congregation for His second coming, Christ seeks to satisfy those people who hunger for a spiritually rich life. Christ seeks Christians who will feed His followers His body that came down from heaven and will reveal the glory of God for all to behold.

Christ calls out, "Live with enthusiasm for me!" Jesus told John to write to the Orthodox Church at Ephesus: "Turn from your sins and do what you did at first" (Revelation 2:5a). To help prepare His congregation for His second coming, Christ seeks to inspire His followers to a life of righteousness and holiness. Christ seeks Christians who will surrender to His lordship and will wear the armor of God's eternal love.

Christ calls out, "Seek the lost for me!" Jesus told John to write to the faithful church at Philadelphia: "I have opened a door in front of you, which no one can close" (Revelation 3:8b). To help prepare His congregation for His second coming, Christ seeks to promote lieutenants to spread the words of salvation through belief in God's only Son. Christ seeks Christians who will brave the battle of axe of Satan himself and will redirect lost souls from the road of darkness to the path of light.

Jesus told His apostles, "The times and occasions are set by my Father's own authority. And it is not for you to know when they will be" (Acts 1:7).

I do not know the day or the hour of Jesus' second coming, but I do know that Christ's church is not ready. I also know Christians everywhere should heed the words of Saint Peter when he wrote:

My dear friends, this is now the second letter I have written you. In both letters I have tried to arouse pure thoughts in your minds by reminding you of these things. I want you to remember the words that were spoken long ago by the holy prophets, and the command from the Lord and Savior which was given you by your apostles. First of all, you must understand that in the last days some people will appear whose lives are controlled by their own lusts. They will make fun of you and will ask, 'He promised to come, didn't he? Where is he? Our ancestors have already died, but everything is still the same as it was since the creation of the world!' They purposely ignore the fact that long ago God gave a command, and the heavens and earth were created. The earth was formed out of water and by water, and it was also by water, the water of the flood, that the old world was destroyed. But the heavens and the earth that now exist are being preserved by the same command of God, in order to be destroyed by fire. They are being kept for the day when godless people will be judged and destroyed.

But do not forget one thing, my dear friends! There is no difference in the Lord's sight between one day and a thousand years; to him the two are the same. The Lord is not slow to do what he has promised, as some think. Instead, he is patient with you, because

John Meacham

he does not want anyone to be destroyed, but wants all to turn away from their sins.

But the Day of the Lord will come like a thief. In that Day the heavens will disappear with a shrill noise, the heavenly bodies will burn up and be destroyed, and the earth with everything in it will vanish. Since all these things will be destroyed in this way, what kind of people should you be? Your lives should be holy and dedicated to God, as you wait for the Day of God and do your best to make it come soon – the Day when the heavens will burn up and be destroyed and the heavenly bodies will melt in the heat. But we wait for what God has promised: new heavens and a new earth, where righteousness will be at home.

And so, my friends, as you wait for that Day, do your best to be pure and faultless in God's sight and to be at peace with him. Look on our Lord's patience as the opportunity he is giving you to be saved, just as our dear friend Paul wrote to you, using the wisdom that God gave him. This is what he says in all his letters when he writes on the subject. There are some difficult things in his letters which ignorant and unstable people explain falsely, as they do with other passages of Scripture. So they bring on their own destruction.

But you, my friends, already know this. Be on your guard, then, so that you will not be led away by the errors of lawless people and fall from your safe position. But continue to grow in the grace and knowledge of our Lord and Savior Jesus Christ. To him be the glory, now and forever! Amen.

2 Peter 3:1-18

Since these early days of Peter and Paul, the church has been directed by its anticipation of Jesus' second coming and maintained by its preparation of His followers to meet Jesus face-to-face in heaven. In light of these church traditions, I ask every Peter and every Paul who call their self a true prophet of Christ:

Is your congregation ready for Jesus' second coming?

And to every Mary Magdalene and every John who call their self a Christian, I ask: Are you ready to meet Jesus face-to-face in heaven?

DREAMS OF THE
SECOND COMING

After this, Jesus appeared once more to his
disciples at Lake Tiberias. This is how it
happened. Simon Peter, Thomas (called the
Twin), Nathanael (the one from Cana in
Galilee), the sons of Zebedee, and two other
disciples of Jesus were together. Simon Peter
said to the others, "I am going fishing."

"We will come with you," they told him.
So they went out in a boat, but all that night
they did not catch a thing. As the sun was
rising, Jesus stood at the water's edge, but
the disciples did not know that it was Jesus.
Then he asked them, "Young men, haven't
you caught anything?"

"Not a thing," they answered.

He said to them, "throw your net out on
the right side of the boat, and you will catch
some." So they threw the net out and could
not pull it back in, because they had caught
so many fish.

> The disciple whom Jesus loved said to
> Peter, "It is the Lord!" When Peter heard
> that it was the Lord, he wrapped his outer
> garment around him (for he had taken his
> clothes off) and jumped into the water. The
> other disciples came to shore in the boat,
> pulling the net full of fish.
>
> John 21:1–8a

The Lord often speaks to us in dreams, and the enemy often attacks us there. I have a friend who once dreamed of the design for the front page of the newspaper where he worked as the assistant graphic director. A few weeks after the dream, he presented the idea to the news editor. In an emotional display, the news editor raved about the design. My friend admitted later that he waited for the perfect time to present this particular design instead of trying to force it earlier. He waited with confidence for the Lord's perfect timing. We must do the same in our lives. Wait for God's timing, even if we need to wait longer in the flesh than we feel necessary, or are willing.

Others have admitted they received the answer for a major life decision in a dream. Many feel a dream was influential in them changing their lifestyle or for getting out of a bad relationship. Some have been visited by loved ones who recently passed away.

Dreams fascinate people. A Google search of "interpret dreams" brought up 1,660,000 sites. That's a lot of sites devoted to helping people understand their dreams. Obviously, not all are Christian.

One year into my life of serving the Lord, I experienced the first of three dreams of the second coming that impacted my life. Twenty-seven years later, while reflecting on these dreams as I enjoyed a relaxing moment on the swings at Frank Liske Park, I uttered four simple words: "Come, Lord Jesus. Come!" Those words, I believe, opened the door for the Lord to reveal to me something far beyond the imagination or understanding of my feeble mind.

In October 1983, I dreamt of Jesus' second coming for the first time. As I slept next to the wall of three windows in one of the "Big House" bedrooms, Jesus flew to earth on a cloud. At least thirty-three meters tall, He stood on a solid gray cloud more than three hundred meters wide. As He descended through a cloudless blue sky toward our bedroom the sun shone off His white clothes, the wind blowing through His hair. This dazzling reflection of the sun's yellow light off His white clothes filled me with memories of the fear that overwhelmed me when I saw the dazzling light in January.

The Lord came within one hundred meters of the room. I awoke, trembling with a cold sweat and a new fear. This fear of Christ not only surprised me but started new revelations and understanding of the nature and hurt our sins. We truly are not worthy, and this became more evident with each dream of the second coming. I learned to put God first, that I was born in Christ, as well as how to grow in Christ, live in Christ, and conquer in Christ

Unable to calm my fear after seeing this glorious vision of Jesus flying through the sky, I slipped out of the bed, careful not to wake my sleeping wife. I moved downstairs for my early morning devotion at three o'clock. I found a Bible in the corner cupboard and sat at the dining room table. I lay my head on the table and prayed for two hours.

My second dream of Jesus' second coming occurred one Saturday night in June 1984 at our home on Wildleaf Court. In this dream, I waited in the front yard of our home and looked up into a cloudless blue sky to see Jesus, dazzling white, riding on a gray cloud. Again, He was gigantic, and I was terrified.

But this time, I was able to brave my fear and watched Jesus shrink in size as he moved closer to earth. When He landed in our driveway, he appeared the size of a normal man.

As I had done when I saw the dazzling light, I knelt on the ground by the dogwood tree in absolute fear. I gazed into His face, which still glowed with the dazzling lights of heaven. He walked to my side, placed His hand on my shoulder, and said, "Do not be afraid. I have work for you to do."

When Christ touched me, I felt the peace that passes all understanding. I felt it in every molecule of my body. My fear dissipated. I knew what He meant to "be brave." I no longer had the strength of a man; I had the strength of Jesus Christ. With that strength, I would follow Him anywhere.

This one moment has motivated me to do His work my entire life.

A week later, I dreamed that I stood on the roof of our house on Wildleaf Court and flew up to meet Jesus on a cloud. As I saw Him from a distance, I was filled with fear and awoke from this dream. I couldn't

John Meacham

handle the fear of flying, much like when Peter walked on water, became afraid, and started to sink. I was in the midst of a physical miracle but was overwhelmed by the realities of this world and forces of gravity. And like Peter, I looked away from Jesus and looked down at the world below.

My third dream, in October 1984, of Jesus' second coming happened again on a Saturday night at the "Big House." In this third dream, I stood waiting by a small green car at the earth and stone stage in the northeast corner of the Sea of Galilee. A large crowd of church leaders had gathered and gazed into a cloudless blue sky. We watched Jesus ride toward us on a white cloud.

When Jesus landed, He talked with the Pope and other church leaders. Much to my surprise, he walked to where I waited for Him in the green Hyundai that I had rented at the Tel Aviv airport. He took a seat in the back. When I looked at Him in the rearview mirror, He said, "I am ready."

We pulled away slowly, careful not to exceed the posted speed limit. I also knew that I must not sin with Christ in the car. As we slipped onto Highway 92, I woke up. It was five in the morning, so I went downstairs and sat at the dining room table for my Sunday morning devotions. I opened my Good News Bible to page 351 and read:

> Then I saw heaven open, and there was a white horse. Its rider is called Faithful and True; it is with justice that he judges and fights his battles. His eyes were like a flame

of fire, and he wore many crowns on his head. He had a name written on him, but no one except himself knows what it is. The robe he wore was covered with blood. His name is *The Word of God*. The armies of heaven followed after him, riding on white horses and dressed in clean white linen. Out of his mouth came a sharp sword, with which he will defeat the nations. He will rule over them with a rod of iron, and he will trample out the wine in the wine press of the furious anger of the Almighty God. On his robe and on his thigh was written the name: *King of kings and Lord of lords.*

Revelation 19:11–16

For many centuries people have predicted Jesus' return to take home His church. A laundry list of those predictions could fill a book. With the Mayan calendar ending in 2012, another wave of predictions has already started to fly.

We also have seen for years the appearance of deceivers, wars, and rumors of wars, famines, great earthquakes, and persecution, all things foretold in the Bible that will usher in the glorious appearing of Christ.

So despite the predictions and signs of the end times, many sadly feel the church as a whole really isn't ready. Part of the reason can be attributed to some pastors thinking the topic of the second coming is secondary to the gospel or even unimportant. Therefore, they don't teach on the topic. Another reason might be that many don't understand the book of Revelation.

John Meacham

Either way, a large number of people do not understand the second coming of Jesus Christ will be the most glorious fulfillment of the gospel since His first coming and the most cosmic event since creation.

To prepare His disciples for His death and resurrection, Jesus told them, "The time is coming, and is already here, when all of you will be scattered, each of you to your own home, and I will be left alone. But I am not really alone, because the Father is with me. I have told you this so you will have peace by being united to me. The world will make you suffer. But be brave! I have defeated the world!" (John 16:32–33).

Just days after Jesus extolled His disciples to "be brave," we read on the shores of Lake Tiberias (also known as Lake Galilee and the Sea of Galilee), they abandoned His mission and returned to their chosen occupation of fishing. These seven fishermen returned to Galilee from Jerusalem filled with fear of the Roman soldiers, fear of the Jewish scribes and Pharisees, fear of Pilate, and fear of the Lord. And to combat this ever gripping fear, they did what most of us do when the going gets rough. They returned to something familiar, something comfortable—fishing.

These same disciples, who now fished in fear off the shores of Lake Tiberias, experienced the details of Jesus' call to them when we read in Luke's gospel that He sent them on a trial mission.

> Jesus called the twelve disciples together and gave them power and authority to drive out demons and to cure diseases. Then he sent

them out to preach the kingdom of God and to heal the sick, after saying to them, "Take nothing with you for the trip: no walking stick, no beggar's bag, no food, no money, not even an extra shirt. Wherever you are welcomed, stay in the same house until you leave that town; wherever people don't welcome you, leave that town and shake the dust off your feet as a warning to them."

The disciples left and traveled through all the villages, preaching the Good News and healing people everywhere.

Luke 9:1–6

Yet on this night at Lake Tiberias, even after seeing the resurrected Jesus twice, these seven disciples sailed out on this all-night fishing venture rather than preparing for mission trips to the many towns in Galilee. Then as the sun was rising, Jesus stood on the northern shore of Lake Galilee. Jesus walked to the water's edge, looked to the south, and saw His disciples fishing in vain. As the sun rose to their east, Jesus said, "Throw your net on the right side of the boat, and you will catch some" (John 21:6).

Jesus then started a fire and began preparing their breakfast of bread and fish. The disciples brought in their 153 fish, and Jesus invited them to "come and eat" (John 21:12).

Before the seven disciples came to the shore of Lake Tiberias with their miraculous catch, Jesus had a breakfast of bread and fish waiting for them. These men had

John Meacham

His power and His authority on earth, and even though they ignored these divine gifts and went out fishing, Jesus did not scold them.

Like me, when I ran away after my first dream of Jesus' second coming, these seven disciples ran away from their unknown divine mission to the earthly work they knew. Yet here in this story of the resurrected Jesus at Lake Tiberias, we see Christ waiting for them, we see Christ waiting for me, and we see Christ waiting for you right here and now. Whenever you are ready, He is waiting—with open arms.

For you, that may mean joining Him at the table each morning. You prefer a different time of the day. That doesn't matter. Whatever time you choose for your daily devotions, Jesus is ready to feed us His eternal food while He reveals to us our mission for the day. And this time spent with the Lord each day in worship and service helps to prepare us to meet Jesus face-to-face in heaven and bring God's kingdom to this world.

In Matthew 4:18–22, we read,

> As Jesus walked along the shores of Lake Galilee, he saw two brothers who were fishermen, Simon (called Peter) and his brother Andrew, catching fish in the lake with a net. Jesus said to them, "Come with me, and I will teach you to catch people." At once they left their nets and went with him.
>
> He went on and saw two other brothers, James and John, the sons of Zebedee. They were in their boat with their father Zebedee, getting their nets ready. Jesus called them,

and at once they left the boat and their father, and went with him.

Peter, the rock, was there at the beginning of Jesus' early ministry in Galilee and he was there at the end of Jesus' earthly ministry. Yet for some reason, Peter needed a threefold reminder of Christ's call to him.

First, "Peter, you are the rock on which I will build my church; go forth and take care of my lambs."

Second, "Peter, you are the rock on which I will build my church; go forth and take care of my sheep."

Third, "Peter, you are the rock on which I will build my church; go forth and follow me—even unto your death on the cross."

Like most of us, after Peter received this firm tongue lashing from Jesus, he pointed his finger at John, the beloved, and asked, "Lord, what about this man?" (John 21:21).

Jesus then told Peter not to worry about John's mission and then once again told Peter, "Follow me!"

In this exchange with His two closest followers, we see that even these two apostles of Jesus Christ are not prepared for the difficult mission He has in store for them. There on the shore of Lake Tiberias, all seven disciples did not appear to understand their mission. Worse yet, all acted like they didn't even know Jesus when they saw Him face-to-face by the open fire where He cooked their breakfast.

Are you ready to meet Jesus face-to-face? Be honest here. No one is looking. Your yea or nay will be only heard by our heavenly Father.

John Meacham

More than likely you said yes, if for no other reason than the shame in admitting you're not. Don't worry. Others are in the boat with you. Most American churches are holding fast to programs and a way of doing things that were established years ago, and thus are failing their congregations. People are seeking—maybe more than at any other time in history. We see this phenomenon in movies, as well as hear it in songs and conversations. Yet by being stuck in a rut with their ways, churches aren't addressing tough issues such as homosexuality, pornography, and adultery. Shame on the church. This must change. It's time for the church to stop dabbling in religion and to grow in spiritual maturity.

On many occasions, I have run away from Christ's righteous and holy path and jumped onto my own road of sin and shame. Yet every time I return to Christ's path, I receive some type of spiritual blessing. One of my richest spiritual blessings came in February 2009 at our final group study class for *Is Your Church Heavenly? A Question from Christ for Every Christian* at First Presbyterian Church in Garner. After we finished discussing the story about the moonlight over Galilee, I handed out hymnals. When all were ready, I started my CD player, and we all sang along with Hayley Westenra as she sang "Abide with Me." After that morning, both now and forever these wonderful words serve as a reminder to me that Jesus is always waiting at our breakfast table and waiting to meet us face-to-face in heaven.

Abide with me! Fast falls the even tide.
The darkness deepens; Lord, with me abide!

When other helpers fail and comforts flee,
Help of the helpless, oh, abide with me!
Swift to its close ebbs out life's little day.
Earth's joys grow dim; its glories pass away.
Change and decay in all around I see;
O Thou who changest not, abide with me!
I need thy presence every passing hour.
What but thy grace can foil the tempter's power?
Who, like Thyself, my guide and stay can be?
Through clouds and sunshine, oh, abide with me!
I fear no foe, with Thee at hand to bless;
Ills have no weight, and tears no bitterness.
Where is death's sting? Where, grave, thy victory?
I triumph still if Thou abide with me!
Hold fast Thy cross before my closing eyes;
Shine through the gloom, and point me to the skies.
Heaven's morning breaks, and earth's vain shadows flee!
In life, in death, O Lord, abide with me!

                                        Amen

John Meacham

CHRIST IN GALILEE

Then I saw heaven open, and there was a white horse. Its rider is called Faithful and True; it is with justice that he judges and fights his battles. His eyes were like a flame of fire, and he wore many crowns on his head. He had a name written on him, but no one except himself knows what it is. The robe he wore was covered with blood. His name is *The Word of God*. The armies of heaven followed him, riding on white horses and dressed in clean white linen. Out of his mouth came a sharp sword, with which he will defeat the nations. He will rule over them with a rod of iron, and he will trample out the wine in the winepress of the furious anger of the Almighty God. On his robe and on his thigh was written the name: *King of kings and Lord of lords*

Revelation 19:11–16

We meet Jesus in many places—most of the time at the cross. It is here that we are to give him our sins—sins that nail him to the cross. Books have been written about these experiences and revelations people have at the cross and the implications on their life.

For me, I met Jesus in my second dream of His return. But I also found out that I was to meet Him again; this time in Galilee.

I always wanted to make a trip to Israel with my wife; me for a spiritual journey and she to visit the various ruins. She and her sister are major history buffs. I thought the two of them might want to add Israel to the places they have visited. But on Father's Day 2003, I discovered I would make this trip alone.

Of course, I received specific instructions of what I was to do while in Israel. Much to my surprise, I was to write a book about the seven churches in Revelation. Like many others, I never considered myself a writer. So for me to write a book I knew it would be totally from and of God.

But I was willing.

So eighteen months later, I drove my 1995 green Hyundai from our home in Raleigh to Dulles Airport in Washington, D.C. Eighteen months can be a long time, particularly when we are forced to wait for something we really want. But think back through your life for a moment. Can you recall something that you really wanted but had to wait for? Were you patient enough to do so? If so, wasn't the reward far greater than you ever expected? That is what happened to me with this trip to Galilee.

John Meacham

Don't get me wrong. I didn't sit idly by, wishing my life away until I had to leave for the trip. I had things to do—specific things. Using a series of numbers (which I soon figured were latitude and longitude), the Holy Spirit revealed where I was to stay. I also had to book airfare and a car rental. And of course, there was the matter of the book. The Holy Spirit instructed me that I was to write a chapter each day about one of the seven churches and in this order: chapter one, Laodicea; chapter two, Pergamum; chapter three, Smyrna; chapter four, Sardis; chapter five, Ephesus; chapter six, Thyatira; and chapter seven, Philadelphia.

In reviewing this order of the seven churches, which differs from the order in the book of Revelation, I noticed the best church, Philadelphia, was last, and the worst church, Laodicea, was first. In my study of these letters, I learned Christ had opened the doors of heaven to Philadelphia and Christ was outside the church at Laodicea hoping someone would hear His call and open the door.

The order in which I wrote is important as it relates to the message to each church. With Laodicea, we are asked to open the doors of the church to Jesus Christ. With the next five churches, we are shown what Jesus Christ wants us to do now that the doors are open. And with Philadelphia, we are asked to open the doors of heaven to the world.

In October 2004, to help prepare for my writing of the book, I taught a series of sermons on the seven churches at Fairview Presbyterian Church in Selma, North Carolina, where I was serving as their supply preacher.

As I finished preaching on October 31, 2004 (the day the time changed from daylight savings time back to standard time), I looked at the clock in the rear of the sanctuary and saw a vision of two in the morning, when the clock actually read noon. While riding home after church, the Holy Spirit revealed the vision was a message the church must change. As our time had changed at two in the morning, the Holy Spirit instructed me the church needed to change from her ways of following Satan and the dictates of the secular world to once again following Christ and the ways of heaven.

Finally the day of my departure arrived: Sunday, January 16, 2005. A myriad of emotions tumbled through my spirit, and, surprisingly, neither joy nor happiness were part of the mix. I felt empty inside and very much alone. To make matters worse, my wife left for church that morning without saying good-bye. Shortly after, I drove my 1995 green Hyundai to Dulles International Airport in Washington, D.C. Without any fanfare, I parked, took the shuttle, passed through security, and boarded my flight. On the outside, I may have seemed like any other passenger headed overseas to Zurich, Switzerland, on that British Airways flight. But on the inside, as I sat in seat 19E, I received signs from the Lord that I was on the right track. During my time as a believer, I learned that the number nineteen is my number for Christ and His church. In my seat, I breathed a sigh of relief when I recognized the number as the Lord's sign that He was directing my journey and that I was now on His clear path to Galilee.

John Meacham

After we landed in Zurich, I made my way to gate E19 and waited to board my Swiss Air flight to Tel Aviv. Three hours later we boarded the plane, and I thoroughly enjoyed the spectacular view of the Alps as we flew south from Switzerland to Israel.

These views of nature's beauty quickly faded when I stepped off the plane in Tel Aviv. I felt lost and alone. I expected a wonderful sense of awe at the prospect of meeting Jesus face-to-face. Sadly and surprisingly, I felt afraid and adrift. Trying to overcome my fear, I pressed forward to the Israeli customs check-in stations. When I reached the front of the line for Station 8, the questions started:

"Why are you in Israel?"

"Why are you traveling alone?"

"Where are you going?"

"Do you know anyone in Israel?"

The check-in official's suspicions grew with each unanswered question. Sensing his apprehension, I found myself getting uneasy. I clearly knew my purpose, but the enemy had slipped into my mind to cause confusion and instill fear. After a moment, I pulled myself together. A list of questions flew through my mind. *How do I answer these questions? Do I tell him that I am following a series of dreams and instructions from the Holy Spirit? Do I tell him that I am here for Jesus' second coming? Do I tell him that I am going to Galilee to wait for Jesus and write a book?*

Just before he called for his supervisor, I mustered up enough courage to tell that I planned to tour Galilee and do some Christian writing. He let me pass, and I went to pick up my 2005 green Hyundai Budget rental car. When I booked the car rental, I had no idea the car would be the same color and make that I owned and drove at home. The assignment of the green Hyundai by Budget was a sign from the Lord that as He guided my path at home, He would guide my path here in Galilee. Also, when I saw the car, I realized it was the same car that I had driven in the third dream of Jesus' second coming.

To compound my problem of feeling empty and alone, I got lost trying to drive out of Tel Aviv. Around three in the afternoon, I found myself lost in one of Tel Aviv's nightclub districts. When I calmed down enough to notice my surroundings, I realized that bars covered the doors and windows of the buildings and many of the citizens wore uniforms and carried guns. After turning down the wrong street multiple times trying to find Highway 20, I pulled into a gas station to ask for directions. I parked the car, got out, and walked toward the station attendant helping a customer.

He suddenly turned around and said, "Do not be afraid. I will help you find your way."

How did he know to speak in English? How did he know I was lost? Why did he say "Do not be afraid?" I have always thought this man was an angel.

Whether man or angel, he calmed my fears and set me on the right path. When finished with his customer, he graciously pointed out Highway 20, which, ironically, could be seen from the gas station. I drove on to Galilee. Finally at 7:15 p.m., I arrived at the Ohalo Manor. The front desk clerk checked me into a room close to the office and restaurant because I was the inn's only guest.

During the night I dreamed that sometime the next day I would start living simultaneously in the two worlds of God's heavenly kingdom and God's kingdom on earth, as I had done when the Spirit of Jesus entered me in April 1985, nineteen years before.

I began my routine the next day of reading Scripture, praying, spending time on the shore of the Sea of Galilee, eating breakfast of fish and bread, visiting "the return site" at nine o'clock to pray for nineteen minutes, touring a holy site nearby, and writing a chapter of *Is Your Church Heavenly? A Question from Christ for Every Christian*. Each day, without fail, I received divine revelations pertaining to the church. Sometimes these revelations shook me to the core. Others caused me to ponder and pray for a while.

The first day, however, I needed to find Jesus' return site, the place of earth and stone that I saw in my dream. I studied my maps and began my quest to find the site of Jesus' second coming. Led by the Holy Spirit, I drove north along the western side of the Sea of Galilee and through Tiberias searching for the spotlights. After turning right onto Highway 92 to drive along the northeast corner, I knew the return site was getting close.

It was the stones.

Large, dark stones lined the northeastern corner of the Sea of Galilee. As I drove past these stones, the Spirit of Jesus entered me. Just as I had in April 1985, I shook with nervous excitement. I pulled off the road at the next overlook to adjust to His presence. After a few minutes of walking outside the car and reminding myself that I had experienced this spiritual indwelling before, I continued down Highway 92 in search of the return site seen in my third dream of Jesus' second coming.

In the distance, I saw, peeking out of the ground like the first sprouts of grass in the spring, the spotlights. At nine o'clock, I turned at the roadside sign marked Daliyyot and parked beside the stage to begin my wait for Jesus to return. I got out of the car and hurried to the return site. Excitement coursed through my veins like a 1,000-volt charge. With the Spirit of Christ indwelled, I thought I could fly as I ran up the steps to the stage for the first time. From the stage, I could see north to the hills of Golan, south to Lake Galilee, east to the fertile groves of banana trees, and west to Tiberias.

Overcome by the Spirit of Jesus within me and the emotion of my dream coming true, I fell to my knees and prayed out loud, "Come, Lord Jesus. Come!" I prayed out loud continuously for nineteen minutes and at 9:19 a.m. closed my offering with the words, "Come, Lord Jesus. Come. The Spirit and the bride say come, Lord Jesus. Come!"

I shook hard that morning, and I felt exactly like I did when I pulled into the driveway and the Spirit of Jesus entered me years before as we drove past the dogwood tree at our home on Wildleaf Court.

Each day the revelations built on the one from the previous and all pointing, guiding each of us to prepare His church for His impending return. The groundwork was laid that first day during my visit to the church at the Mount of Beatitudes. As I entered the church, the sanctuary's striking interior design and immaculate cleanliness brought me to a state of reverence and respect. I knelt at a prayer station, bowed my head, and noticed a paper bag placed on the floor near my knees.

I picked up the bag and saw written:

Open Doors
Ezekiel 7:12
Isa. 29

When I returned to my room at the Ohalo Manor, the Spirit of Jesus instructed me to study these two passages. The words from these passages and the letter in Revelation to the church of Laodicea caused to me realize one thing: Christ wants a church that is white hot.

> To the angel of the church in Laodicea write: This is the message from the Amen, the faithful and true witness, who is the origin of all God created. I know what you have done; I know that you are neither cold nor hot. How I wish you were either one or the other! But because you are lukewarm, neither hot nor cold, I am going to spit you out of my mouth! You say "I am rich and well off; I have all I need." But you do not know how miserable and pitiful you are! You are poor, naked, and blind. I advise you, then, to buy gold from me, pure gold, in order to be rich. Buy also white clothing to dress yourself and cover up your shameful nakedness. Buy also

some ointment to put on your eyes, so that you may see. I rebuke and punish all whom I love. Be in earnest, then, and turn from your sins. Listen! I stand at the door and knock; if any hear my voice and open the door, I will come into their house and eat with them, and they will eat with me. To those who win the victory I will give the right to sit beside me on my throne, just as I have been victorious and now sit by my Father on his throne. If you have ears, then, listen to what the Spirit says to the churches!

Revelation 3:14–22

Specifically look at what John wrote in the following verses:

I know what you have done; I know that you are neither cold nor hot.

Revelation 3:15

But because you are lukewarm, neither hot nor cold, I am going to spit you out of my mouth!

Revelation 3:16

But you do not know how miserable and pitiful you are!

Revelation 3:17

John Meacham

And why is that? Simple! "The time is coming. The day is near when buying and selling will have no more meaning, because God's punishment will fall on everyone alike" (Ezekial 7:12). And from the passage Isaiah 29, we read in verse 13:

> These people claim to worship me, but their words are meaningless and their hearts are somewhere else. Their religion is nothing but human rules and traditions, which they have simply memorized. So I will startle them with one unexpected blow after another. Those who are wise will turn out to be fools, and all their cleverness will be useless.

Christ wants His faithful followers to open the doors of His church so the poor and humble might once again find happiness in the Lord. We can't do this by sitting on a sofa or in a recliner. We must get up, get moving. The gospel says to *go out* and make disciples. Most people won't take the time to enter a church across the street from their home, even if invited. People need led in—with love, kindness, and compassion. Then, and only then, when they are ready, will they join the armies of heaven. But we have to do our part first.

Once the doors are open and Jesus has returned, repentance is important. For without repenting of our sins, we cannot serve as Christ's soldiers. The letter to the church in Pergamum states this clearly.

To the angel of the church in Pergamum write: This is the message from the one who has the sharp two-edged sword. I know where you live, there where Satan has his throne. You are true to me, and you did not abandon your faith in me even during the time when Antipas, my faithful witness, was killed there where Satan lives. But there are a few things I have against you: there are some among you who follow the teaching of Balaam, who taught Balak how to lead the people of Israel into sin by persuading them to eat food that had been offered to idols and to practice sexual immorality. In the same way you have people among you who follow the teachings of the Nicolaitans. Now turn from your sins! If you don't, I will come to you soon and fight against those people with the sword that comes out of my mouth. If you have ears, then, listen to what the Spirit says to the churches! To those who win the victory I will give some of the hidden manna. I will also give each of them a white stone on which is written a new name that no one knows except the one who receives it.

Revelation 2:12–17

On this day, my second of writing, I observed groups from three continents—Europe, Asia, and Africa—being baptized at Yardenit, the ceremonial site of Jesus' baptism on the Jordan River. One group, Ethiopians, after rising up from the water, rushed to the rock wall and shouted praises to the Lord. When they reached the wall, they dropped to their knees and continued to praise Jesus.

Writing about Pergamum proved a most difficult task. Needing more time than the previous day, I consumed large amounts of coffee and wrote well into the night. The lesson learned from that day is that Satan works overtime trying to lead Christians away from the holy waters of baptism into the darkness of sin. Christ instructs His repentant followers to turn from their sins and to become people of the light.

My reading the next day took me to the letter to church in Smyrna.

> To the angel of the church in Smyrna write: This is the message from the one who is the first and the last, who died and lived again. I know your troubles; I know that you are poor—but really you are rich! I know the evil things said against you by those who claim to be Jews but are not; they are a group that belongs to Satan! Don't be afraid of anything you are about to suffer. Listen! The Devil will put you to the test by having some of you thrown into prison, and your troubles will last ten days. Be faithful to me, even if it means death, and I will give you life as your prize of victory. If you have ears, then listen to what the Spirit says to the churches! Those who win the victory will not be hurt by the second death.
>
> Revelation 2:8–11

Later that day, while at the return site, I saw a small white stone. I picked up the white stone, read my new name etched on the white stone, thanked Jesus for His help, put the white stone in my pocket, and started praying "Come, Lord Jesus. Come."

When I wrote that day, an easier task for sure, the Spirit of Jesus led me to Psalm 121.

> I look to the mountains; where will my help come from?
>
> My help will come from the Lord, who made heaven and earth.
>
> He will not let you fall; your protector is always awake.
>
> The protector of Israel never dozes or sleeps.
>
> The Lord will guard you; he is by your side to protect you.
>
> The sun will not hurt you during the day, nor the moon during the night.
>
> The Lord will protect you from all danger; he will keep you safe.
>
> He will protect you as you come and go now and forever.
>
> Psalm 121:1–8

From this passage and the words to the church of Smyrna, we learn Christ instructs His true followers to look to the hills and rejoice in His victory. He also illuminates the path to spiritual riches through honest worship, through fervent prayer, and through His Father's Word.

John Meacham

Christ drove home a key point the following day when He left me to my own vices. And boy did I mess up big time. I ended up in Tiberias to dine at McDonald's, my first chance to be "American" since arriving in Israel.

After washing down my cheeseburger and French fries with a super-sized Coke, I returned to my car and discovered a parking ticket under the windshield wiper. Oops. I had not noticed the small self-pay parking booth at the end of each row.

Now, I was scared! I couldn't read the parking ticket, and I started to imagine all sorts of negative outcomes that could befall an American who had broken a law in Israel. Unable to sleep upon my return to Ohalo Manor, I finally realized I was here in Galilee serving my Lord Jesus Christ and if I had to suffer some negative consequences for my actions, then that would be okay. I then prayed, "Thy will be done."

That experience and reading the following provided some insightful revelations from the happenings of that day:

> To the angel of the church in Sardis write: This is the message from the one who has the seven spirits of God and the seven stars. I know what you are doing; I know that you have the reputation of being alive, even though you are dead! So wake up, and strengthen what you still have before it dies completely. For I find that what you have done is not yet perfect in the sight of my God. Remember, then, what you were taught and what you heard; obey it and turn

from your sins. If you do not wake up, I will come upon you like a thief, and you will not even know the time when I will come. But a few of you there in Sardis have kept your clothes clean. You will walk with me, clothed in white, because you are worthy to do so. Those who win the victory will be clothed like this in white, and I will not remove their names from the book of the living. In the presence of my father and his angels I will declare openly that they belong to me. If you have ears, then, listen to what the Spirit says to the churches!

Revelation 3:1–6

I realized that we often use the church to pursue our own dreams of financial security and personal pleasure. The church in Sardis had the reputation of being alive to world (i.e., lots of programs at church to make people happy) but was dead to the spirit. Sound like some churches today? Of course it does. Do you attend a church that is more focused and interested in helping you pursue the physical aspects of life and not becoming alive to Christ? For example, teaching a Dave Ramsey class on finances to help bring in new members is a disguise for using the lure of making more money to increase their membership.

How wrong is that?

That night in Israel I became alive to the world and went to find the world's pleasure in food at McDonald's. Because of my transgression, the Spirit of Jesus left me

John Meacham

from the time I fed my gluttony until I paid my fine and returned to the earth and stone stage for my nine o'clock prayers.

Each day brought new revelations—some stronger than others. Some days, like the fifth day of writing, I had to really ponder what had been revealed.

> To the angel of the church in Ephesus write: This is the message from the one who holds the seven stars in his right hand and who walks among the seven gold lampstands. I know what you have done; I know how hard you have worked and how patient you have been. I know that you cannot tolerate evil people and that you have tested those who say they are apostles but are not, and have found out that they are liars. You are patient, you have suffered for my sake, and you have not given up. But this is what I have against you: you do not love me now as you did at first. Think how far you have fallen! Turn from your sins and do what you did at first. If you don't turn from your sins, I will come to you and take your lampstand from its place. But this is what you have in your favor: you hate what the Nicolaitans do, as much as I do. If you have ears, then, hear what the Spirit says to the churches! To those who win the victory I will give the right to eat the fruit of the tree of life that grows in the Garden of God.
>
> Revelation 2:1–7

During my visit to St. Peter's Memorial Church, I had the opportunity to observe a Catholic mass. While one of the priests preached on the familiar story of the resurrected Jesus' third appearance to His disciples in John 21:1–14, a terrible storm moved in over the Sea of Galilee. A group of tourists sought shelter in the church, but the nun chased them out. Then, to my horror, she locked the fence so they couldn't get back in. All of this happened while the priest shared how Christ took care of the disciples by fixing their breakfast.

Back in my room, I studied the fishing story passage in John's Gospel and the Spirit of Jesus reminded me that, unlike what I saw at St. Peter's Church, the gate of His love was always open, and He waits every morning to feed spiritual food to all of His followers.

With three days to go, I felt both exhausted and exhilarated.

> To the angel of the church in Thyatira write: This is the message from the Son of God, whose eyes blaze like fire, whose feet shine like polished brass. I know what you do. I know your love, your faithfulness, your service, and your patience. I know that you are doing more now than you did at first. But this is what I have against you: you tolerate that woman Jezebel, who calls herself a messenger of God. By her teaching she misleads my servants into practicing sexual immorality and eating foods that have been offered to idols. I have given her time to repent of her sins, but she does not want to turn from

John Meacham

her immorality. And so I will throw her on a bed where she and those who committed adultery with her will suffer terribly. I will do this now unless they repent of the wicked things they did with her. I will also kill her followers, and then all the churches will know that I am the one who knows everyone's thoughts and wishes. I will repay each of you according to what you have done. But the rest of you in Thyatira have not followed this evil teaching; you have not learned what the others call "the deep secrets of Satan." I say to you that I will not put any other burden on you. But until I come, you must hold firmly to what you have. To those who win the victory, who continue to the end to do what I want, I will give the same authority that I have received from my Father: I will give them authority over the nations, to rule them with an iron rod and to break them to pieces like clay pots. I will also give them the morning star. If you have ears, then, listen to what the Spirit says to the churches!

Revelation 2:18–29

During Sunday worship at the Church of the Multiplication of the Loaves and Fishes, a priest gave most of the liturgy in German but near the end said in plain English, "The people living in darkness have seen a great light."

Then almost immediately, he said, "On those living in the land of the shadow of death a light has dawned."

Both times I responded with a hearty, "Amen!"

From the message that morning, preached from Matthew 4:12–23, Jesus revealed that the righteous should follow the lights of heaven and bring forth the kingdom of God. Banded together, we are equipped to join the armies of heaven and save the lost. Christ solicits His chosen followers to join the armies of heaven and remain faithful and true to His leadership. Christ commands His loyal followers to join the armies of heaven and conquer the world for Him.

Before I began my last day of writing, the Spirit of Jesus reminded me of what He had said to Martha before He raised Lazarus from death: "I am the resurrection and the life. Those who believe in Me will live, even though they die; and those who live and believe in Me will never die" (John 11:25).

What an incredible call to arms. How can we not see the call to gather the troops for battle?

That morning I read:

> To the angel of the church in Philadelphia write: This is the message from the one who is holy and true. He has the key that belonged to David, and when he opens a door, no one can close it. I know what you do; I know that you have a little power; you have followed my teaching and have been faithful to me. I have opened a door in front of you, which no one can close. Listen! As for that group that belongs to Satan, those liars who claim that they are Jews but are not, I will make them

come and bow down at your feet. They will all know that I love you. Because you have kept my command to endure, I will also keep you safe from the time of trouble which is coming upon the world to test all the people on earth. I am coming soon. Keep safe what you have, so that no one will rob you of your victory prize. I will make those who are victorious pillars in the temple of my God, and they will never leave it. I will write on them the name of my God and the name of the city of my God, the new Jerusalem, which will come down out of heaven from my God. I will also write on them my new name. If you have ears, then, listen to what the Spirit says to the churches!

Revelation 3:7–13

Disappointed by a boring visit to Jesus' town that day, I headed for the exit. In the bushes that grow atop the wall that surrounds Capernaum, I saw a peacock displaying its plumage there among these ruins. In Byzantine and early Romanesque art, the peacock served as a symbol for Christ and the resurrection. I took his picture and returned to my room to write.

In that moment, I understood that Christ wants His eternal followers to join the armies of heaven and save the lost. Christ wants His chosen followers to join the armies of heaven and remain faithful and true to His leadership. Christ wants His loyal followers to join the armies of heaven and conquer the world for Him.

How then can we not answer the call to gather the troops for battle?

As I lay in bed that night, I felt unprepared and unqualified, like I still do to this day, to spread this message from Jesus Christ to a world that *does not* want to hear from Him.

The night I left this incredible journey, one in which I experienced many incredible highs, emotionally, physically, and spiritually, I made one last trip to the earth and stone stage. A spectacular full moon illuminated the northern sky over the hills of Golan. I opened the windows, turned on the interior lights, and read in Revelation where John reported:

> Then I saw heaven open, and there was a white horse. Its rider is called Faithful and True; it is with justice that he judges and fights his battles. His eyes were like a flame of fire, and he wore many crowns on his head. He had a name written on him, but no one except himself knows what it is. The robe he wore is covered with blood. His name is *The Word of God*. The armies of heaven followed him, riding on white horses and dressed in clean white linen. Out of his mouth came a sharp sword, with which he will defeat the nations. He will rule over them with a rod of iron, and he will trample out the wine in the winepress of the furious anger of the Almighty God. On his robe and on his thigh was written the name: *King of kings and Lord of lords*.

> Revelation 19:11–16

John Meacham

As I read, the interior became the site of a furious windstorm. Then, at 6:21 p.m., the alarm sounded on my wrist watch for nineteen seconds. I looked one last time at the return site. I had not set the alarm, so I considered it as Jesus' farewell to me at Lake Tiberias. In that instant, I realized that every moment in my life had prepared me for this moment and that every moment for the rest of my life would be lived to make this message from the King of kings known to the world.

As I drove along the eastern shore of the Sea of Galilee, I was awestruck at the full moon reflecting the sun's light into the dark night sky. I continued my drive, going past the big fisherman that sits atop these eastern hills of Galilee. At that time, the Spirit of Jesus left me and returned to heaven. I then prayed, "Christ in me. Christ in the world. Amen."

THE ARMIES OF HEAVEN

By reading through this book, one would assume you are an excellent candidate to join the armies of heaven. However, assuming anything about anyone is a dangerous proposition. The choice is yours and only yours. Your spouse can't make that decision for you or your boss or your mother—only you.

Do you hear Jesus Christ calling into the churches with His words of recruitment?

It's time—time for His people to recognize His call, to recognize the need to get ready, to get ready to prepare a battle the likes of never seen before in the history of mankind.

Jesus Christ calls for recruits who are born again. Like with Nicodemus, our spiritual birth, or rebirth, leads to a new life of trying to follow God's will, and I still pray each morning that He will keep me on this wondrous path to His Glory.

"Jesus answered, 'I am telling you the truth: no one can see the kingdom of God without being born again'" (John 3:3).

Jesus Christ calls for recruits who hear God speaking to them. I believe God speaks to us daily. To fully hear Him, our spiritual antennas must be up. We must be willing to put down our own agenda and listen for the loud and clear voice of the Lord.

"The Lord has done this, and it is marvelous in our eyes" (Psalm 118:23, NIV).

Jesus Christ calls for recruits who accept Him as their Lord and Savior. While street preachers and door-to-door salesmen—err, I mean evangelists—often focus on getting people to say the sinner's prayer, accepting Jesus as your personal Savior involves much more than saying a prayer. We must confess our sins, believe in His life, believe in His death, and believe in His resurrection.

"For God loved the world so much that he gave his only Son, so that everyone who believes in him may not die but have eternal life" (John 3:16).

Jesus Christ calls for recruits who will reflect His holy light. Unfortunately, many churches today are reflecting the wrong thing. We see their love of money and idolatry among the numerous rays of tainted light. Christ is seeking those who wholly reflect His goodness and love.

"The dazzling light passed through the east gate and went into the temple" (Ezekiel 43:4).

Jesus Christ calls for recruits who will help Him sing the songs of heaven. To sing His praises, we must first be willing to be used by Him. So when we cry out "use me, oh Lord," do we really mean it? Do we allow the Holy Spirit to indwell us and then sing Christ's praise and do Christ's work?

"But when the Holy Spirit comes upon you, you will be filled with power, and you will be witnesses for me in Jerusalem, in all of Judea and Samaria, and to the ends of the earth" (Acts 1:8).

Jesus Christ calls for recruits who will follow Him into the war for His church. Our fight is not against the flesh, although some days it may feel that way and we counter with an offensive in the flesh, but rather against powers and principalities. After we encounter Jesus Christ, are we willing to rise up off our sofa or even off our favorite church pew and become a soldier in His army?

"After this, Jesus appeared once more to his disciples at Lake Tiberias" (John 21:1).

Jesus Christ calls for recruits who will fight to reform His church.

> Then I saw heaven open, and there was a white horse. Its rider is called Faithful and True; it is with justice that he judges and fights his battles. His eyes were like a flame of fire, and he wore many crowns on his head. He had a name written on him, but no one except himself knows what it is. The robe he wore was covered with blood. His name is *The Word of God*. The armies of heaven followed him, riding on white horses and dressed in clean white linen. Out of his mouth came a sword, with which he will defeat the nations. He will rule over them with a rod of iron, and he will trample out the wine in the winepress of the furious

anger of the Almighty God. On his robe and on his thigh was written the name: *King of kings and Lord of lords.*

Revelation 19:11–16

Jesus Christ needs dedicated Christians to help Him form heavenly churches and conquer the world in His name. If you are interested in joining the armies of heaven and fighting to reform Christ's church, please send me an e-mail to john@dazzlinglight.org.

John Meacham

ENDNOTES

Born Again

1   Barclay, William. *The Daily Study Bible Series: The Gospel of John, Vol. 1.* Philadelphia, Pennsylvania: The Westminster Press, 1975 (First Published in 1955). pp 124-128

2   Meacham, Jon. *The End of Christian America.* Newsweek.com. April 13, 2009

3   Meacham, John. *Is Your Church Heavenly? A Question from Christ for Every Christian.* Canton, Michigan: Zoe Life Publishing, 2008. pp 49-51

God Speaks

1   "100 Thing Challenge: Living with just 100 Items in Your Life." *Neatorama.* http://www. neatorama.com/100-thing-challenge. August 27, 2009

Accepting Jesus

1   Ruis, David. *The Worship God is Seeking.* Ventura, California: Regal Books, 2005. pp 20

Jesus Sings

1   Osteen, Joel. *Become a Better You.* New York, New York: Free Press, 2007. pp xi